MEDITATION

Path to the Deepest Self

MEDITATION

Path to the Deepest Self

Michal Levin

Foreword by Ken Wilber,
author of A Brief History of Everything

DK Publishing, Inc.

London, New York, Sydney, Delhi, Paris, Munich and Johannesburg

Senior Designer: Mandy Earey
Category Publisher: LaVonne Carlson
Creative Director: Tina Vaughan
Cover Art Director: Dirk Kaufman
Designer: Diana Catherines
.Production Manager: Chris Avgherinos
DTP Designer: Russell Shaw
Picture researcher: Jo Walton

To my beloved co-creator

First American Edition 2002

2 4 6 8 10 9 7 5 3

Published in the United States by
DK Publishing, Inc.
375 Hudson Street
New York, New York 10014

Dorling Kindersley Publishing offers special discounts for bulk purchases for sales promotions or premiums. Specific, large-quantity needs can be met with special editions, including personalized covers, excerpts of existing guides, and corporate imprints. For more information, contact Special Markets Department, Dorling Kindersley Publishing, Inc., 95 Madison Avenue, New York, NY 10016 Fax: 800-600-9098.

LIBRARY OF CONGRESS CATALOGING-IN-PUBLICATION DATA

Meditation: path to the deepest self / Michal Levin.
      p. cm.—(Whole Way Library)
Includes index.
ISBN 0-7894-8333-5. (alk. paper)
1. Meditation. 2. Vizualization. 3. Healing.
I. Title: Meditation: Path to the deepest self.
II. Title. III. Series. .

BF637.M4 L48 2002
158.1'28—dc21

2001047747

Color reproduction by Colourscan, Singapore
Printed and bound in China by L.Rex Printing Co.Ltd
See our complete catalog at
www.dk.com

CONTENTS

ENERGY 14

UNDERSTANDING ENERGY 16

THE ENERGY BODIES 40

There is a secret, a rather extraordinary secret, that has come down to us through the ages, that has been whispered in the forests by visionary shamans, counseled quietly in mountain temples by ancient sages, guarded by the awakened ones who are said to have plumbed the very depths of the human and the Divine. This secret has rumbled down the valleys, cascaded through the hills, caught the wind by surprise and sent all who heard it weeping with awe.

FOREWORD

Some say this ultimate secret unlocks the mysteries of life and death itself, that it points directly, unmistakably, to a hidden road that miraculously leads from time to eternity, from death to immortality, from bondage to freedom, from the human to the radiant Divine… finding which, one has found All. In the past, this secret has been mightily guarded, a nuclear power that in the wrong hands could spell disaster. Guarded also because, quite frankly, it takes a very special person to be able to even see it, or recognize the staggering, shuddering power it can unleash: a power that trumps death is nothing to bandy about carelessly, is it? Only in isolated, sacred, lonely grounds has this secret been whispered from master to student, a finger over the lips. "Shhhh…. Tell only those who are ready," was the sagely advice.

It is one of the great ironies of the modern world that, exactly at a time that many would consider the most forlorn, the most abandoned, the least spiritual, the least meaningful—only in the modern world has this secret therefore been released from its cloistered estate and been made available to those who have the ears to hear and the eyes to see and the heart to respond.

Well, then, the secret? It comes in three parts, the sages say. One: Spirit does indeed exist. Two: Spirit is not a God out there but a Self in here. Three: The royal road to that Spirit within is meditation.

And, the sages add, in such an extraordinary venture, on such a miraculous journey, please choose your guides with care.

My friend Michal Levin is such a guide, and the book you now hold in your hands, *Meditation: Path to the Deepest Self*, is a superb introduction to this ultimate secret, the secret of how to find who and what you truly are… in the deepest, highest, part of you. For the great sages East and West are unanimous about one, fundamental, earth-shattering fact: the very deepest part of you intersects, and is directly one with, the all-pervading Spirit of the universe at large. There is indeed a God: that God is looking out of your eyes right now, reading the words on this page right now, holding this book in its hands, right now. And meditation is a way to realize that truth, to awaken to that ever-present Reality, to honor that ultimate secret of the universe that will indeed lead you from time to eternity, from death to immortality, from bondage to liberation… in this simple moment, and in this simple moment, and in this.

Are you ready to begin that extraordinary journey? Well, my friends, you have come to the right place, and with all my heart I wish you Godspeed on this remarkable discovery.

Ken Wilber
Author of *A Brief History of Everything*.

Meditation is a profound mystery, like a door into another reality that is always there but cannot be seen. For years I knew nothing about it, and cared less. I didn't hear the prompting. I took no notice of the signs. I didn't choose meditation. But, in despair, looking for something else, I stumbled upon it. By its extraordinary, hidden power, meditation became the route that led me into a wider, deeper world—or to the further reaches of this one. Meditation is the path that led me to my innermost self.

NTRODUCTION

t the same time, meditation is the path that eads to the place where the mysteries of the niverse reside and the keys to existence wait. It is hard to put those experiences into vords. No words seem adequate; most sound wkward. Meditation is the place where I first ound the most complete knowledge of God or the force I call God) and myself, and where learned how the two are both the same and ifferent. And meditation also saved my life, terally (but more of that later).

Many practices go by the name of neditation. This book is about the meditation echnique I know best and have taught over he past ten years. (It is the basis of a diary bout my journey, which became a book, *The ool of Memory: The Autobiography of an Unwilling ntuitive*.) This meditation technique brought ne the kind of "knowing" that is often called intuition" and much else.

I learned this technique when I did not think t was possible, when I was not interested. I ad sampled much the world had to offer and known a great many joys, but I still felt an agonizing incompleteness, an undefined longing. I was in pain. The dark night of the soul that enveloped me seemed formless and endless, but no one could see it on the outside.

I was competent, caring, in charge, and concerned. I took care of my children, pursued my work (as a current affairs television reporter on primetime, national TV), mourned the breakup of my marriage, saw friends, went to parties…and descended into an inner abyss. Looking up, I saw no way out. Far, far above I saw light—a hole, but a hole full of light. I did not know how to reach it.

Like a spider's web, a frail ladder brushed my face. "You should meditate, it would be easy for you," a healthcare professional remarked. I brushed the suggestion aside impatiently, as if it were a spider's web—of no substance or significance. I lived in the world of facts, social justice, compassion even, not mysticism.

As the months slipped by, my incomprehension deepened. I found it difficult to say what was wrong. Life simply did not add up. It was not enough, but it was too much. I did not understand... or maybe I understood too much? I did not want because I did not know what to want. Impatient and distracted, like a petulant child, I decided one evening to give meditation a try "just to prove it wasn't for me." That night ten years ago utterly and irreversibly changed my life.

I followed the instructions I had been given, expecting very little to happen. (To be honest, just the thought of meditation bored me!) Instead, I felt as if the sky opened, as if the universe expanded ten million times, as if nothing I had ever dreamed of and everything I could hardly conceive of converged on me. Another reality opened and embraced me.

In the months that followed I was forced to recognize my intuitive (some use the word "psychic," which I dislike) and healing abilities. I was taught by the inner world— or is it an outer or extended one?—to see a quality I can only call "energy," and then I learned to understand the meaning of what I could see. I gained a much deeper and sometimes very different understanding of people, events, and the world. I gained the ability to see into the hearts of those who came to see me (an ability used then, and now, only when others ask for help). This awareness changed my experience of life, and the Universe, in almost every way. And I changed too.

Most importantly, the changes inside me brought a quality of Love I had never dreamed of. I discovered an understanding and experience of Love that encompasses ethics, morality, and truth. It also brought what I can only call "a knowing." Suddenly I knew so much, but much of that knowledge seemed altogether unimportant.

At the same time, being the skeptical, tried, and tested journalist that I was, I kept detailed notes of what was happening to me. I had to. That was part of the initial instruction I received in my earliest meditation: Write it down. Strangely, I had excellent recall, even after the longest meditation sessions. As the weeks became months, my meditation diaries grew.

Soon people began to seek me out, asking for my help, whether I liked it or not. In the beginning, I doubted whether I had anything to offer. I was utterly suspicious of assuming I had any ability, of assuming anything except that "my" meditation was totally compelling for me.

I am not a Buddhist, but it was a high Tibetan lama who first spotted, and insisted, that I had a gift. Soon after that, people started to seek me out for consultations. Their numbers quickly swelled. Professional people—psychotherapists, business people, creative artists, teachers, IT specialists, even celebrities, as well as representatives of most walks of life—filled my diary, and formed a waiting list. That was ten years ago.

Since then my ability to work with, and understand, energy has steadily increased, along with my understanding of the Universe and life. This ability has brought help and healing to many others, as well as myself. I have learned and taught much more than I can put into words. My work, my meditation,

INTO THE DEEPER DOMAIN
*A picture created during the period I was spending
much time in intense meditation*

and my awareness of energy also have brought me peace, humility, and an understanding of the Universe and my place in it that I otherwise would never have held, truly, in my heart.

That "knowing" also saw me through the most perilous times that lay ahead, when my life hung by a thread, with physical death and disfigurement beckoning. Three years after beginning to work as an intuitive, while instructing a meditation group, I happened to see my own energy, something that rarely occurred.

In my mind's eye I saw the right-hand side of my body as dark, and the darkest area of all was at my head. I knew the condition was deeply ingrained from the fact that though I could dispel the darkness by directing healing light at it, it very soon returned. It was definitely something that was already in my body, and which I could not disperse by healing energy alone. If I had seen those signs in a client, I would have urged my client to consult a doctor immediately. I knew what I had to do.

I went to see my doctor and several others, alternative as well as orthodox. Everywhere I went I drew a blank. No one could explain

UNIVERSAL PATHWAY
*This painting represents the way
humans are interconnected.*

At last, when I felt death was very near (though no one else remotely agreed), the inner voice of my meditation led me back to my birthplace, South Africa. It instructed me to find one particular doctor there, identified only as "the rose grower." Amazingly, he was easy to find—there was an eminent doctor well-known as a "rose grower."

In his hospital office with a glorious view of Table Mountain, that irascible, engaging doctor, wearing shirtsleeves and no white coat, uncovered a suspected brain tumor, on my right-hand side. His discovery proved correct. I was about to die as a result of a huge tumor. I had weeks, a few months at best, to live. (Later I learned that the tumor had grown slowly throughout most of my life; probably having been caused by an experimental X-ray treatment in childhood.) It was a "benign" tumor, an acoustic neuroma. But because of its position and its size—as big as a peach according to the brain scan—it was about to take my life.

my condition. No one could find anything wrong with me. Instead, they frequently sent me away with explanations, each one different, that I knew were not true: "The after effects of hepatitis, previously experienced," "A spiritual problem," "Mercury fillings in your teeth," "Post viral fatigue"—all these suggestions were among their responses.

Very soon after its discovery, I underwent an operation at a center of excellence for this surgery at The House Clinic in Los Angeles. The tumor was removed and my life was saved, but at a cost I lost my hearing on one side and my facial nerve was severed, with all the consequences that implies: an eye which could not shut, half a mouth which could not move, loss of feeling, and more.

All the time, though, my meditation and
eality, as I came to know it through meditation,
ept me grounded. In the months that followed,
my ability to work in an intuitive capacity
(which I had speculated might be lost) became
even stronger. However, the form of my work
changed and the scope of my understanding
widened. And through the years since, my
physical recovery has progressed, slowly,
steadily, and very successfully.

I was not "cured" by an overnight miracle. My
tumor was not removed by an act of "God" or
some spiritual invocation. It was removed by
scalpel. But never for a moment did I let
go of my spiritual practice, or my spiritual
reality—nor did it let go of me. In that way,
experienced a miracle, and continue to do
so. That "knowing," which held me through
my darkest hour, continues to hold and teach
me now. In everyday life, for example, it shows
me the intense pleasure of a morning sky, a
quiet street at night, or simply the exuberance
of a weed caught in a cracked paving stone. It
helps me constantly to learn and understand,
by experiencing it, how all beings are part of
one another and the Universe. And the start
of it all was meditation.

Meditation and the gifts it brings have been
route to joy, and more, for me and for many
have taught. At the same time, meditation
and what followed have transformed the
elements of joy and understanding for
me. I feel joy where I did not before. I also
understand when I did not before. The quest
for truth, peace, right action, and wisdom has
deepened to penetrate, enfold, and inspire me
in everyday life.

This journey will continue all the days of
my life, even when the practice changes. I have
been privileged to help many others find this
route map and to explore in this way. I offer
my experience to my readers here. The form
of the events and consequences I encountered
along my journey was special to me, just as
the events and consequences each individual
encounters are special to him or her. Each
encounters a different world. Each says what
he or she sees in his or her own words. But
the essence is the same: peace, unity, and
enduring Love.

> Not all of the following techniques are
> suitable for everyone. I cannot say that this
> technique is ideal for every person and will
> definitely do him or her good. This is the
> technique that brought "the other world"
> to me, and has helped many I have taught.
>
> Each person must take responsibility
> for the consequences if he or she chooses
> to try it. If one has any mood-related,
> emotional, or nervous problems, a history
> of such problems, or takes drugs for an
> emotional or other condition, do not try
> this technique without asking the advice
> of a medical practitioner.

1
ENERGY

How to start meditation? How to
cut through explanations varying
from the mystical to the magical?
How to satisfy the rational mind
while awakening the deeper forces ?
I start with the word "energy"—a
word that used to horrify me when
used outside the dictionary sense.
Now I *recognize its importance.*

In the old traditions, the most powerful

meditations were often kept secret.

For example, Dzogchen (the highest

path in Buddhism) and Tantra (ancient

practices involving sexual rites, yoga,

and meditation) in both Hinduism and

Tibetan Buddhism were reached only by

adepts after long spiritual journeys, and

then held as closely guarded secrets.

UNDERSTANDING ENERGY

The practitioners who worked with such ancient traditions knew the immense power of meditation and the spiritual teachings around meditation practices. These methods have the power to influence one's life, experience, and actions.

Different kinds of meditation aim to achieve different effects. For example, one variety tries to still the mind and bring peace by banishing all thoughts. Another aims to attract the blessings or powers of a particular deity.

The meditation I teach is unique. It depends on understanding the concept of "energy"—one's own energy and that of the outer world—in a particular way. It is based on the premise that one can change his or her energy. Specifically, one can purify and expand one's energy, and by doing so, change his or her feelings, reactions, and behavior.

In order to learn how my aproach to meditation works, it is important first to understand what I mean by energy. This section on Understanding Energy explains the many meanings behind the word "energy," and how they all come together to represent a force that flows through one's life and all of the universe. Becoming aware of how everything is interconnected creates new insights, perspectives, and opportunities.

THE WAY OF THE WORLD
An energetic landscape

WHAT IS ENERGY?

Energy is the wind in the trees, it is the sweetness of a smile, the silence of falling snow, the release of laughter, the glint in a stream, the sprint to the finish line. Read it in the imprint of feet on the sand, feel it in the rocks on the seashore, hold it in your hands as it courses through the body. Energy is in everything.

The energy of the wind has forced the trees to bend in its path.

Einstein defined energy as $e=mc^2$. Energy equals matter multiplied by the speed of light, squared. In other words, all matter can be described as a form of energy. In scientific terms, energy is a spectrum made up of frequencies. All events, as well as all matter, fall along that spectrum.

The energy of objects and of events can be described in different ways. Cardiologists register the beat of the heart as an energy-generated signal, an index of life and well-being. It can be heard and also recorded as an image on an electrocardiogram (EKG or ECG). What is being perceived and measured is electrical energy. With the appropriate equipment, it can be picked up

om any cell in the body. However, another
rce, described as electromagnetic energy, also
manates from the heart. By using even more
ophisticated techniques, cardiologists can pick
o this electromagnetic frequency as much as
ght to ten feet away from the body.

As frequencies along a spectrum, all types of
nergy merge into one another. The wavelengths
f chemical, magnetic, and electrical bands of
nergy overlap, with considerable variation within

each band. For example, the sound of a dog
whistle is inaudible to humans but not to dogs!
Humans hear only part of one end of the
frequency. What humans perceive using all of their
senses is a small part of a vast picture. So much
more exists—it is everywhere—and it can never
be destroyed. It can be transformed, deflected, or
distributed in many different ways, but it cannot
simply cease to exist. The implications of the
indestructibility of energy are enormous.

SEEING ENERGY IN A NEW WAY

When I first began to see energy, I felt I was seeing
something that could not "be there"—yet I could
see it. And somehow I understood what it meant!
What I saw offered me information, extraordinary
as that seemed. This experience happened at a
painting class, during my sabbatical when I was
trying to find a way to deal with my inner disquiet.

Our skilled painting teacher,
Sandy, asked the class to paint
a model who was sitting for us,
using only two colors. I chose
blue and yellow and began
painting, concentrating very
hard as I am not trained in life
drawing. But standing back, I
realized I had painted a small
red patch at the model's elbow
I had done it without thinking,
automatically painting what
I saw.

Sandy was intrigued. "It
takes attention away from the
proportions of the arm, which
aren't quite right," she said. "That red patch
deflects the eye." As I saw what I had done,
I understood simultaneously that it meant the
model was experiencing pain at his elbow. I
was utterly taken aback by this realization.

SEATED MALE NUDE

I could not explain why I had painted the red
patch—except that I could see it, which in itself
was extraordinary. I had even less idea why I
should imagine I knew what it "meant." When
I tried to put a word to what I could see, the
one that seemed most appropriate was "energy."
That was the start of my seeing, and later working
with, energy. Now when I work
as an intuitive, I believe I "read"
my clients' energy, as many
other intuitives do.

Is this notion of energy related
to the concept of energy used
in the realms of science? I do
not know. But, it is clear that
science itself does not have
complete answers to the
questions posed by energy.

For example, exactly what
is the role of electromagnetic
energy in the body? Where does
it come from and what causes
it to change? Though medical
science does not have the precise answers to
these questions at the moment, doubtless it
will. Sooner or later, the relationship between
the way I use the word energy and scientists'
understanding of it will become clear.

INFORMATION & ENERGY

Most people understand that the trace of a heartbeat is an energy-generated signal, and that the beat carries information. Morse code works on the same principle. Similarly, when a human voice is recorded, the recording can appear on a screen as a series of traces marking frequencies.

Everyone "reads" information from energy-inspired events around them, though they may not think of energy in quite that way. Cooks understand the information offered by a temperature gauge on an oven. Wind surfers or sailors know the exact difference between gale force one and gale force seven winds. Examples abound of how one constantly picks up information from or about energy.

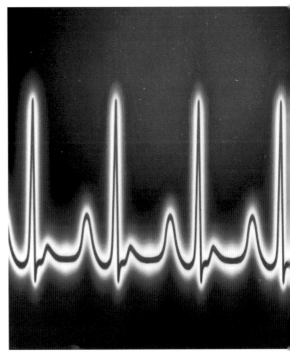

Silent and unseen, the flow of energy through the heart can be measured and displayed in the graphic traces of each heartbeat.

The effects of energy are cumulative. Where one blow may not fell a tree, several blows will. One knock might not harm a glass table, but ten knocks in the same place might cause a crack.

he matter the table is made of (which is
timately condensed energy) holds and stores
he traces of each of the knocks until, under their
ombined pressure, it cracks. In that way, energy
eates, and holds, a history. This principle—
at energy creates and holds a history—is
nportant, especially when considering places
nd, particularly, in regard to the human body.
Many different examples demonstrate the
ea that the past is registered.The rings of a tree
gister its age. As they grow, the nails may register
ness or physical problems by developing ridges.
In the same way, thoughts and feelings make
mark. In some areas, experts clearly accept
at feelings affect physical health, even to the
xtent of creating or enabling disease. If that
so, then a cross-over point must occur when
o much of a certain feeling or thought may
ctually become a physical symptom. That point
specific to each person and depends on his or
er individual traits. Overall, feelings, thoughts,
nd experiences register and are held. Life
roves that for most people.

If someone is consistently rejected in love,
e or she is likely to approach affairs of the heart
ith a different attitude and in a different spirit
an someone who has been well-loved and had
history of romantic success. If one has a track
cord of athletic achievement, his or her
nfidence before a race is likely to be greater
an that of someone who has never placed in
event. So, in the same way as experiences
gister in memory, I believe their mark can also
e described in another way: They leave a trace
one's energy.

What marks one's energy, though, is not only
ovious events, thoughts, and feelings. For
xample, everyone is aware of odd occasions
hen they know who is going to be on the other
nd of the phone before they pick it up. How?
lucky guess? Or telepathy? I suggest describing

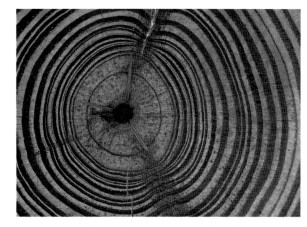

*Tree rings provide an obvious example of how the
past is registered. Although humans do not acquire
visible "rings" to show their age, their energy holds
the marks of their development.*

the phenomenon in another way, as a sort of
energy transaction. As someone makes contact
by placing the call, the other may pick up the
information as an energy message.

Something similar certainly occurs with
animals. In his book *Dogs That Know When Their
Owners Are Coming Home and Other Unexplained
Powers of Animals*, biologist Rupert Sheldrake
used carefully controlled experiments to find
overwhelming statistical evidence that some
dogs know in advance when their owners are
coming home, despite having no conventional
explanation for this knowledge. One dog
demonstrated in repeated random experiments
that he sensed when his owner phoned a taxi
to bring her home.

Clearly the pets in these experiments were
responding to something, but what? The answer
could be "intention." One way to understand
intentions could be to consider them as energy
signals: The owners' intentions of coming home
are transmitted energetically to their pets. This
concept—that energy both registers events and
transmits information—is very important in
understanding and using the meditation I teach.

THE ENERGY OF OBJECTS & PLACES

When meditating, everything around—even what one wears or sits on—affects the results.

Just as a place of beauty can lift or affect one's spirits, a room where people have argued can carry a negative "atmosphere." In meditation one becomes more open to the various influences of the environment, so that where one chooses to meditate is particularly significant.

SEA OF LIFE
An energy picture of land and water

Places themselves hold energy. Everyone has observed an animal avoiding a particular corner fo some inexplicable reason. Some environments are enormously pleasing while others create quite different feelings.

Feng shui is the Chinese discipline based on a set of theories about the energetic forces that occur in every location, and how changing these forces can affect the lives of those who live there. In that way, feng shui and the meditation technique I teach here has some similarities. My technique is based on the idea that by purifying and expanding one's own energy, one can help change his or her behavior.

Apply this principle to matter. Because matter can be thought of as condensed energy, it means that all objects are energy. Instinctively, one knows that a favorite pebble has a special feel.

room panelled in wood looks and feels warmer than a room lined in steel. Architects, designers, and artists often have a highly developed sense of these qualities of materials. Their senses are not simply "aesthetic," they mirror a reality that affects everyone. This is especially significant when one tries to open and expand the senses during meditation.

According to beliefs associated with the American Indian Medicine Wheel, rocks and minerals have a special ability to hold energy. Many cultures around the world share the view that water has great powers of purification.

From my experiences with clients, I have found that wood is particularly good for absorbing fear and offering reassurance. Sitting on a wooden chair produces a subtly different effect than sitting on a metal chair. Stone is grounding, but unyielding. Earth has a hugely supportive effect. Walking barefoot strengthens everyone.

Water is especially important. It has wonderful qualities for absorbing or washing away vibrations, including negativity. Think of how uplifting a waterfall can be. I like to have a large vase filled with fresh water near me when I work. I advise everyone to shower or bathe, if at all possible, before meditating.

These ideas are common (although expressed in different ways) to various systems of thought, from Chinese philosophy to the Medicine Wheel of American Indians. Medicine Wheel theory teaches that rocks and minerals hold energy, and that plants give energy and animals receive. But while the animal in humans receives, humans are the only beings with the potential for full self-determination in how to deal with energy.

As well as having intrinsic energetic qualities, objects also acquire the energy of their surroundings or of the people who use them. Mediums often ask to hold something belonging to their sitters or to those with whom their sitters want to connect. Aside from mediums, the comfort that can come from an object or piece of clothing that belongs to a loved one is well known. A client recently told me that she could not wash the shirt she was wearing when she first embraced her soon-to-be partner. Perhaps the reason for this reaches beyond sentimentality.

When visiting the Holocaust Museum in Washington, D.C., I was overwhelmed by the agony I sensed emanating from the piles of clothes of gas chamber victims, accompanied by a low gray haze. I sensed clearly that their original owners' energy clung to the clothes and added to the museum's horrors.

ENERGY & COLOR

Color is an important aspect of one's surroundings. Sunlight contains all the colors of the spectrum, each vibrating at a particular energetic frequency. At the same time, those different frequencies carry more information than simply the color itself. Colors affect both feelings and physical responses—a concept that leads to a number of uses and implications.

Until the past century the vast proportion of people worked outside, exposed to natural light and thereby to the full energetic spectrum. Nowadays, many people are deprived of natural light for much of the day, thus are deficient in the energy provided by full spectrum light.

The use of light is recognized as a treatment in medicine for a depressive condition caused by sunlight deprivation, known as seasonal affective disorder, or SAD. It works by encompassing the full spectrum of sunlight to compensate for shortages in winter months.

The rainbow, a symbol of harmony, covers the full spectrum of light.

OLD WOMAN OF THE HILLS
The orange represents a flare of human energy in an environment that is mostly green and hilly.

Color, rather than simply light, is widely used to improve everyday situations. For example, red traffic lights are not just a convention. The color red is recognized as attracting attention to itself, unlike a peaceful blue, which encourages emotional harmony. Hospitals often use a pale green shade, especially in operating rooms, because green acts as an antidote to red blood and also promotes a peaceful subdued feeling. Artists and designers are familiar with the idea of warm colors and cool colors, and how they affect viewers' moods.

These and more detailed theories of color are the basis of color therapy, a specialized form of alternative healing, where colored lights, silks, and other materials are used to treat both physical and emotional conditions. It's worth remembering that color is truly an alternative source of energy.

INTERPRETING COLOR

The energy of color is a valuable resource. Every color has a unique significance, although interpretations may vary from individual to individual and from situation to situation. Culture, history, and geography may influence the use of particular colors. In ancient China, yellow was considered a celestial color.

In primitive socities, where only dyes obtained from local materials could be used, available plants and minerals determined color choices. History aside, in a contemporary society an individual's reaction to a color may be a reaction to the issues or areas that the color symbolizes.

For example, green often represents balance, harmony, freedom, adaptability, renewal, and peace in its positive form. It's negative form can signify envy, jealousy, or selfishness. A dislike of green may relate to one's feelings about being in balance or having a sense of peace. Perhaps the dislike implies a sense of being out of balance or not feeling at peace. Alternatively, it can indicate a dislike of selfishness or even a fear of jealousy.

Precisely what the reactions to a color indicates depends on an analysis of each individual situation. But in general terms, reaction to a color indicates a reaction to the feeling states—positive or negative—associated with that color. At the same time, remember that reactions change. Today's preference may not be tomorrow's. Situations change, and color can play a part in influencing change.

Generally colors cannot be considered as good or bad, higher or lower. Rather, they are keys to unlocking greater insights about one's mood or state of mind. And, of course, they can be keys to changing those factors.

COLOR	POSITIVE	NEGATIVE
red	Power, passion, sexuality, warmth, interpersonal love, affluence, the physical, impulsiveness, exercise of will (the ability to ask or demand), courage.	Brutality, lust, resentment, obstinacy, war, anger, danger.
orange — Combination of red and yellow	Vitality, energy, revitalizing, enterprise, enthusiasm, assertiveness, creative, fun.	Exhibitionism, overbearing, destructive.
yellow	Cheerfulness, wisdom, confidence, balanced approach, intellect, reason, logic, optimism.	Flattery, deception, malice, selfishness, vindictiveness, calculating, controlling.
green — Combination of yellow and blue	Balance, harmony, freedom, adaptability, understanding, peace, renewal, vitality.	Envy, suspicion, grievance, injustice, jealousy, stagnation, selfishness.
turquoise — Combination of yellow and blue	Transformation, transition, youthfulness, freshness, uplifting, change.	Cold, isolated, confused, immature, unrealistic.
blue	Serenity, spirituality, coolness, renewing (linked with water), faith, devotion, trust, reliability, power of service.	Disbelief, laziness, depression, doubt, excess ambition.
violet — Combination of red and blue	Intuition, overview, integration, self-respect, nobility, fluency, vision, tolerance.	Intolerance, forgetfulness, impatience, isolation, pride, superstition, corruption.
magenta — Combination of red and violet	Regal, integration, efficiency, reverence, idealism, grace.	Despotism, self-obsession, disregard.
pink — Combination of red and white	As a shade made by combining red and white, pink can carry a special quality of universal love.	Powerlessness, selfishness, self-absorption.
white	White is not the absence of color, but the presence of all colors—it contains all possibilities.	By containing all possibilities, white includes the capacity to be negative as well as positive.
black	Black is an absence of color. It may represent avoiding issues—benefits and complexities—of color. It also may function as a form of protection.	Depression, inability to embrace life, desire to control the environment and the self within it.

ENERGY & SOUND

Sound does more than simply please or offend according to personal taste. Sound, like light, is composed of frequencies. Over the ages, searchers and scientists have not only measured the frequencies of sound, but have also tried to relate them to the frequencies of light or even a cosmic order. Although sound and light exist in different frequency ranges, as energy they have similarities.

Sound, like light, plays a fundamental part in shaping the world. The New Testament says, "In the beginning was the Word," which refers to the primary significance of God's word. But it also suggests that sound itself, which is composed of energetic frequencies, played a fundamental part in the beginning of existence.

The Old Testament emphasizes the power of sound in the story of the fall of Jericho when the walls of the city were shattered by the sound of trumpets. It also tells of King Saul's deep depression being lifted by music. David played the lyre to him and "he was refreshed and the evil departed." King Saul may have felt rid of his "evil" by the aesthetic beauty of the music, but something deeper was also going on: The incident was an energetic interaction.

In the development of Western thought, the Pythagoreans, in the sixth century B.C., gave music numerical equivalents as a way of measuring the energy of sound. They saw these numbers as the basis for a complex, far-reaching universal system. The Pythagoreans believed that earthly music was a faint echo of the universal "harmony of the spheres." To the ancients the cosmos was a series of planetary spheres ascending from Earth to Heaven, like the rungs of a ladder. Each sphere was thought to correspond to a different note of a grand musical scale. Thus, music, sound, and, specifically, the frequency of the sound was the underpinning of the entire cosmos. (In later years, in medieval Europe, this system was even used as a basis for architecture.)

Buddhism holds a number of similar ideas. For example, the syllable "Hung" is one of the main so-called "seed syllables," or sounds that ct as precursors to the manifestation of Buddhist eities. Expressions known as "mantras," a form f chant, are also used to invoke or call up articular deities or powers. Described as "vajra ords" (*vajra* means "indestructible"), they are elieved to have special powers referred to as "the nergy of truth." The power of a mantra does not

way. In very advanced practices, natural sounds, like the sound of falling rain or thunder, become part of preparing for experiences after death.

Another very important Buddhist concept, transmission, is the belief that wisdom or insight, and the power it confers, is passed by direct contact—even in the form of the sound of the

ibetan Buddhist priests use ceremonial sound in the belief that the
esonance and vibration of the sound aids in fulfilling the ceremony's function.

eside simply in the meaning of the words, but in he sounds themselves. Repeated use of mantras ver time increases their power. Mantras are hought to embody the indestructible (vajra) nergy of enlightenment.

Buddhists use special exercises for what is alled "purifying speech" to cleanse the effects f "impure expressions," such as undesirable vords one may have uttered. The exercises involve epeating vowels in a particular time-honored

teacher's voice—from teacher to student. This contact enables communication on other levels, including thought and meditation. In other words, transmission sets up an energetic link that is often carried through the voice.

This principle applies to anyone who uses their voice. In terms of energy, sound conforms to a particular set of frequencies that have their own effects, beyond the strict interpretation of words.

THE POWER OF SOUND

Sound and healing have a long association. Tibetan religious rituals make a special place for sound. Their bells, which are like metal cups that come in many shapes and sizes, are used specifically for healing. The theory is that the sound of the bells, particularly their resonance when played, has the power to affect the body's energy and to heal it.

The Christian tradition does not seem to have a parallel, but singing the daily offices forms the framework of life for many Christian monks and nuns. In their case, perhaps the human voice acts as the voice of the spirit or the vehicle of spiritual healing.

Certain Tibetan Buddhist rituals use bells, based on the belief that their resonance has a healing effect on the body.

Recent medical research suggests that music stimulates the release of various chemicals in the body, including endorphins (the brain's pain killers). The therapeutic use of music is well-established and even used in hospitals. Neurologist Oliver Sacks, M.D., states: "I regard music therapy as a tool of great power in many neurological disorders—Parkinson's and Alzheimer's—because of its unique capacity to organize or reorganize cerebral function when it has been damaged."

...onasteries like this one were homes to the many nuns and monks who gave their ...es to God. Often their days were structured around singing the Lord's praises.

Many experts in other health fields, from critical ...re to immune system functioning to autism, ...gree on the power of music. Music therapy is ...sed to help those with mental illness, elderly ...ersons, and children with special learning needs. ... these instances music is used to strengthen ...on-musical areas such as communication and ...hysical coordination skills.

The tremendous destructive potential of sound ...ust also be recognized. From the workplace ...o the dance floor, over-exposure to loud noise ... a common cause of deafness. Also, music's ...ower to affect the emotions can lead to abusing ...s power. St. Augustine (AD 354–430) warned ...gainst that danger:

The mind ought never to be given over to and enervated by this physical delight, for it often beguiles me in that the perception of the senses is not attended by reason. The senses do not so attend on reason as to follow her patiently, but rather, having gained admission for her sake, they strive even to run on before her and be her.

Individual variations and responses play a significant part in the effects of sound. Sounds from one section of the frequency range are not necessarily more powerful in a particular way than those from another. They are powerful in different ways. They also have varying effects on each individual at different times. Indeed, aesthetic taste may relate to variations in an individual's energetic state or requirements.

What emerges clearly is that the energy of sound has the power to interact with one's mental and physical states. I believe that sound also affects the spiritual. St. Augustine puts forward this idea when he talks about Psalm 32 and contemplates the meaning of a "jubilation"—a song or sound like "alleluia":

What does singing a 'jubilation' mean? It is a realization that words cannot express the inner music of the heart. For those who sing in the harvest field, or vineyard, or in work deeply occupying the attention, when they are overcome with joy at the words of the song, being filled with such exaltation, the words fail to express their emotion, so, leaving the syllables of the words, they drop into vowel sounds—the vowel sounds signifying that the heart is yearning to express what the tongue cannot utter.

Sound carries its own powerful energy. And when the human voice is used to create sound, that power goes beyond the meaning of the words. When first working with a group, I was repeatedly perplexed when trying to record a session: Nothing would record. I eventually understood that the energy of our sessions was too fine for an ordinary tape recorder. Finally, supersentitive professional equipment caught the sound of my voice.

ENERGY & SMELL

Touch, sight, sound, taste, and smell make up the five senses. In approaching meditation, all the senses are significant. Though it may seem that the fundamental mechanics of smell are different from those of light and sound, they actually share important features. Like the other senses, smell and taste are highly sensitive, subject to individual variation, and affected by how they are used.

For example, overpowering the sense of smell by exposure to a smoky atmosphere makes it more difficult to pick up other smells. Technically, when smell occurs, an odor molecule meets with an odor receptor in the nose. This is not simply a chance meeting, an all or nothing phenomenon. The "receptor coupling," which is the technical term, depends on the vibrational frequency of the molecules to create bursts of nerve activity

Babies and mothers alike quickly learn to recognize and feel comforted by each others' scents.

like morse code. This pattern of activity, which transmits the information, can be measured like any other frequency. In short, the energy of smell is measurable and carries information.

Babies recognize their mothers' smell and mothers recognize their babies' smell. Research suggests that children can distinguish between the smell of their siblings and that of other children of a similar age. Emotions can be ommunicated by smell: Dogs and horses are receptive to the smell of fear in humans. Memory and smell are closely linked, as many remember encountering a childhood smell that instantly brings back the past. Clearly, smell is an enormously important transmitter and receptor.

From my own practice, I know the power of smell and its uses both in strengthening the ability to be receptive and in transmitting information about others and the environment. But while smell can be useful in heightening the senses or in helping to transmit information, it can also disable the capacity completely. I regularly see cases where overuse of strong smells, such as essential oils, leads to a type of nervous burnout that can be difficult to overcome.

When leading group meditations or advising on meditation practices I always stipulate: No perfume, no aftershave, no strong smells, and no aromatherapy, unless one is certain of how to use them. I also recommend washing, if possible, before beginning.

This cautious and respectful approach to smells is even reflected in the New Testament Book of Revelations, "The four beasts and twenty elders fell down before the lamb, Having every one of them harps, and golden vials full of odours, which are the prayers of saints."

Eastern traditions encourage the use of incense. When trying the meditation I teach, unless one has superior information on precisely which type of incense and exactly how much to use, I recommend avoiding it.

All of the old religious traditions have recognized the power of smell, and developed herbs and plants for special purposes. Below are four of the best known. If trying them, be very careful with the quantity used: Less is more.

SACRED SCENTS

SAGE is used in the American Indian tradition to clear spaces. The Romans called sage a "herba sacra," a sacred herb. They believed it strengthened the senses and memory.

ROSEMARY, among the earliest plants to be used for magic, was considered sacred in many civilizations. Sprigs of rosemary were burnt at shrines in ancient Greece. In the Middle Ages they were used to drive away evil spirits.

ROMAN CHAMOMILE was used by the ancient Egyptians for mystical purposes. The Moors used it in a similar way. For the Saxons it was one of nine sacred herbs; they called it "maythen."

TRUE LAVENDER is well-established in many folk traditions as a restorative. Of particular relevance here, it is believed to act as a nerve tonic and stimulant.

ENERGY & FOOD

What one takes into the body through the mouth is just as significant as what one experiences or consumes through the eyes, ears, and nose. Food is not simply calories. It is matter, condensed energy, that burns in one's body to provide fuel. It has been used across the world, through the ages, as medicine and even as a conduit for elements of spirituality.

The understanding that food has a deeper significance comes in many guises. In anthropology, one explanation of why cannibals ate their enemies was their belief that they incorporated the enemies' strength. Native Americans searched for particular plants in order to imbibe their energy. Ayurveda, the traditional Indian medicine, uses food as medicine.

The Christian belief that spirit can be imparted into matter is represented in the communion bread and wine.

A leading ayurvedic practitioner in the West, Dr. Vashant Lad, describes the spiritual and energetic powers of food: "The Creative energy in food is Brahma; the nourishing energy in food is Vishnu; the transformation of food into pure consciousness is Shiva. If you know this then any impurities in the food you eat, will never become part of you."

The Christian idea that spirit can be imparted into matter is prominent in communion bread and wine. The bread and wine represent the body and blood of Christ, which the communicant absorb by swallowing. The physical substances are transmuted by association and intention, as the poet John Mansfield wrote in "Pompey the Great":

The corn that makes the holy bread
By which the soul of man is fed,
The holy bread, the food unpriced,
Thy everlasting mercy, Christ.

pinions differ on whether the bread literally
ecomes the physical body of Christ or symbolically
presents Christ or, by extension, the community
f God—all those involved in the making of the
read and the wine. The central idea remains that
he food represents—and holds power as—more
an simply itself.

In Buddhist practice, special pills known as
mrita, or dudtsi, perform a similar function.
he amrita are prepared by mixing together so-
alled precious substances, often including jewels
nd herbs, and then saying mantras over them
 give them the powers invoked by that particular
antra. These pills are then given as a form of
lessing at the end of ceremonies, retreats, or
her occasions—a clear example of the belief that
 substance can carry non-physical properties into
e body when swallowed.

Like all matter, food is affected by the elements
hat contribute to its makeup and circumstances
hat contribute to its existence. For that reason, I
onsider homegrown food easiest to digest because
s vibrations are the same as one's environment
nd community.

Macrobiotic theory avoids food imported
om a long distance (particularly if it comes from
 location due north or south). Macrobiotic theory
lso warns against food eaten out of season, due
 the notion that the body is part of a larger
hole and includes all aspects of the environment,
uch as the season of the year. Promoting the
reatest degree of harmony means balancing the
ody within the environment. For example, if one
ves in Boston and eats South African peaches
 December, the body is forced to assimilate a
omplex vibrational pattern. Conditions surrounding
e growing, harvesting, and preparation of food also

Homegrown food may be easiest to digest because its
vibrations align with those of one's environment.

play a part. The moral superiority or desirability of a
vegetarian diet is not a hard and fast rule. In talks
given in London in 1984 and 1986, the Dalai Lama
expressed his belief that vegetarianism is admirable
and his appreciation that the number of vegetarians
is increasing, but revealed that after contracting
severe jaundice in the 1960s he was advised by his
physician to discontinue vegetarianism. He
maintains that under certain circumstances a diet
that includes meat is necessary.

Both ayurveda and macrobiotic food theory
allot a role to animal products as food. Clearly,
personal circumstances dictate this issue. But
the energy carried in the carcasses of factory-
farmed animals must reflect an element of their
existence that is absorbed when they are
eaten—a sober thought. Eating food grown,
reared, cooked, and prepared with care and
eating in loving circumstances always provide
the best nourishment. Those who are especially
concerned with color feel that the color of a food
is important too.

All this is relevant to meditation, because the
practice is about awakening sensitivity, which is
promoted by awareness and consideration of all
issues. Before meditating, avoid eating a heavy
meal. But hunger serves no purpose, so do eat
something light.

ENERGY & PEOPLE

In all of life, nothing may be stronger than the effect we have on one another. People are often inspired by others. The smell of a lover's clothing brings a host of memories. A harsh voice shrivels one's soul. As the lips touch a baby's downy head, the scent evokes other childhoods, past and present, and the special, sacred quality of new life.

EMBRACE
Human embrace

Patterns learned from key figures in childhood, and possibly further back, play themselves out over and over again throughout one's adult years. In so many ways, people rule one another's lives, creating each other's realities. By a complex web of chemical substances, emotional ties, and intellectual rules, people interact ceaselessly. Each discipline describes this dance in its own way, including psychology, physiology, philosophy, physics, chemistry, and others.

The body itself is a hugely powerful energetic instrument—transmitting, receiving, and recording. Each step of the dance is recorded in one's energy. Each emotion, thought, experience, and intention is transmitted and stored in a particular way. Just as objects carry energy and experience, people who are infinitely more complex, also carry energy.

To further complicate the picture, each person carries an energetic heritage, a blueprint, similar in a way to one's genetic makeup. That heritage is composed of many factors that influence the individual, including family circumstances, the past, places, individual traits, and more. Sometimes one understands this heritage and sometimes one does not (or not for a long time).

Coming to know one's energetic heritage means, in psychological terms, becoming whole and aware. In more spiritual terms, it can mean uncovering the soul's purpose or letting the light shine through. In essence, this awareness is about allowing one's being to manifest in all its splendor and to bring the blessing of connection to the universe. To achieve that end, one must travel through the maze created in relation to all the other people in one's life. When doing so, ignoring the power of others' energetic influence is perilous.

Surroundings influence one in myriad subtle ways. The senses are capable of registering a host of impressions one may not instantly recognize. The complexities of one's experience are held in the energetic body. The people one associates with may infuse themselves into one's energy in ways that are not recognized until later.

Psychology teaches that special dynamics occur in groups. These association with others leave marks and create their own patterns. One cannot help feeling the effect of the energy of all those he or she spends time with—parents, teachers, friends, lovers, children, colleagues, and others.

The I Ching, the Chinese book of wisdom, warns of friendships or close relationships:

He *finds a comrade,*
Now he beats the drum, now he stops.
Now he sobs, now he sings.

This vacillation is an example of what happens when one's source of strength lies outside oneself, in relationships. If one's center of gravity depends on others, even in benevolent close relationships, one is tossed in an almost random process between joy and sorrow, rather than experiencing feelings coming directly from one's own core. This possibility warns against being influenced too much by others, and advises choosing friends and associates carefully.

This vulnerability raises the issue of what can happen when the influence behind an association is actively destructive. As inner strength develops, the opportunity for associations, based on real trust and love, increases, leading to stronger, wiser, more fulfilling relationships. In developing inner strength, one may encounter the power of energy patterns held in the body since childhood. These patterns can draw one repeatedly into painful or destructive situations that may require therapeutic help. While children are dependent and subject to the energy of those around them, adults have a responsibility to monitor those effects and address the patterns that occur.

Knowledge and awareness are the keys to making choices. They bring privilege and a responsibility to choose companions wisely. The meditation technique I teach offers a chance to change the patterns held in one's own energy. Opening oneself in the way necessary to enable change can leave one particularly susceptible to outside energetic influences. If one meditates in the company of others, choose those companions carefully. As understanding deepens, one may feel the need for different companions. A greater life beckons.

THE ENERGY OF THE BODY

The energy of living bodies is fascinating and brilliant in its complexity. The energy of the human body has two main aspects. The first is the energy within the body, a common concept. The second is the energy emanating from the body, just as celestial or mythological beings are said to emanate radiant light.

A TRANSFORMATION
The energy I felt washing over my face in sleep

Humans, like all material bodies, emit energy. This energy around the body is an essential part of transmitting who an individual is. A person's energy gives off all kinds of information about him or her and what he or she is feeling. It also holds a record of one's history and progress. In the same way that objects and places hold their history, so the energy of the body holds one's stor Whether it is held in the form of an actual imprint from an event, or as the effect of thoughts and feelings pertaining to the event, is irrelevant. The end result is the same.

As energetic beings, people are affected by their history and retain the imprint of that history—until or unless it is erased by some

Among the various types of energy in the body, the finest energy is associated with spirituality. Depending on how the inner energies are developed or disrupted, they can help cause the physical body to grow stronger or to become ill.

method that is not simply a device to suppress it. Meditation can be a method of erasing, or improving, old imprints.

The meditation I describe is specifically aimed at that process. It is designed to help eradicate the negative historical traces held in one's energy and, by purifying that energy, to help in the process of expanding and transforming it. In that way, one's essential being is revealed, along with its unfettered connections to the greater universe.

The movement of energy and the process by which it is organized follow clear rules. The physical vehicle, one's flesh and bones body, is very dense, highly compact energy. As that energy extends outside the body, it becomes finer and finer. Energy is a spectrum: One state bleeds into another. The energy outside the physical body can be divided into roughly three bands known as the "subtle energy bodies."

Generally, energy moves from the outside, from the finest bands, in towards the physical body. For example, in registering one's experience, a particular distressing incident could be held repeatedly in the finer bodies, until, eventually—if one did not remove its imprint—it would move into the physical body and create an actual physical problem. To develop to one's fullest and expand all of one's capacities, an individual needs to be able to clear the obstacles from all aspects of his or her being—spiritual, mental, and emotional. This need to clear obstacles is why it is so important to understand the mechanics of energy.

The subtle energy bodies are like three

layers that enclose the vulnerable physical

body. The quality of each layer's energy is

different and acts in a unique way. Energy

moves from the outside in towards the

body. The overall picture is similar to the

energetic event that takes place when

lightning strikes. It occurs in stages.

THE ENERGY BODIES

The first event in the occurrence of lightning takes place at an electromagnetic level, hidden from any sort of human observation. The second event is a sound—the characteristic crackle—that expresses a different frequency. Then the flash occurs, which is the expression of the frequency that shows light. Finally, as the flash strikes the ground, a searing interaction takes place with the physical energy of the earth. In this way, what is described as "lightning" is actually three or four separate phases of an energetic process, each with distinct characteristics. Similarly, an individual's energy is, in a sense, spread over four phases: the spiritual, mental, emotional, and physical.

Human energy can be understood as working in the same way as lightning—with one major difference. With individuals, the ability of one part of the system to affect the whole is of crucial

TRANSFORMATION 1
The yellow lines have been superimposed on my picture to give an idea of the energy bodies.

importance. Overall, the human energy system is a finely balanced, interdependent system. If one part of the system is unbalanced, it distorts the whole.

This connection between the energy bodies makes understanding them and their interactions vital. For example, developing the spiritual body is impossible if the emotional body is obstructed. So a childhood hurt held onto and retained in one's energy blocks spiritual development, as it skews perceptions and understanding. Or if one's mental body is distorted, perhaps by a conviction that the non-physical is irrelevant, that imbalance affects both emotional and spiritual development.

When one understands the importance of developing and balancing the energy bodies, the path forward becomes clear: If one aspires to grow as a complete human being, one cannot compartmentalize oneself.

THE SPIRITUAL BODY

The spiritual body, the name given to the energy body furthest away from the physical core, is the subtlest of the four. This energy is of the finest quality, which is one reason why it eludes some people for so long. The spiritual body is the domain of spirit and also of intuition. Movement in this realm is faster than the speed of light. It is the flash of inspiration, the knowing of intuition, the certainty of trust immediately recognized.

Plato compared a unified soul to the power gained when the strength of steeds was combined with guided thought. Likewise, a person with unified energy bodies is able to accomplish great achievements.

Those spiritual impulses and knowing need to move through the other energy bodies to reach the physical, where they can be translated into personal choice and inform action. Only when one's spiritual energy reaches the physical body can actions be informed by spiritual beliefs that are deeply and truly held, rather than by trends, emotional needs, or self interest of some form. The power of one's spiritual energy is limited by the energetic obstacles blocking its influence. To prevent those obstructions, the history held in all of the energy bodies must be transformed. Once the pathway along which energy travels is relatively free of obstructions, the energy of spiritual knowing can move effectively into the physical body.

This 19th-century print depicts Joan of Arc, the young Frenchwoman whose visions inspired her to lead soldiers into battle for a holy cause during the 15th century.

The idea that spiritual development does not depend on a single factor alone was expressed in earlier times, in different ways. For example, in *Phaedra*, Plato spoke of the soul as a unity of forces, liable to fly apart: "Let the soul be likened to the union of powers in a team of winged steeds and their winged charioteer." In other words, the spiritual dimension of humanity is a unity of forces.

SPIRITUAL LEADERS

Fortunately, one can look throughout history to examples of men and women whose spiritual energy has been well developed, though to different degrees and in various ways. Ghandi, Martin Luther King, Mother Theresa, and Nelson Mandela provide a few recent examples of prominent individuals who have been driven by spiritual ideals. Of course, countless other men and women sincerely aspire to live good lives and help their fellow beings and the universe.

Mohandas Gandhi's nonviolent revolution helped India gain freedom in 1947.

Martin Luther King, Jr., was a key leader in America's civil rights movement in the 1960s.

Nelson Mandela, a leading rights activist in South Africa, became its first black president in 1994.

Mother Teresa of Calcutta won the Nobel Peace Prize in 1979 for her humanitarian work as a nun in India.

THE MENTAL BODY

The next energy body is the mental, or intellectual, body, where thought takes place. This energy is not as fine or quick as spiritual energy, but is faster than that in the bodies that follow. In energetic terms, one requires sustained mental and emotional development to open the pathways to spiritual understanding—an idea that has been repeatedly recognized over time.

From the ancient Greeks to the relatively recent Renaissance, great thinkers have valued the idea of fullness and unity. Though earlier cultures did not identify emotion in the way it is today, the predominant belief was that harmony, power, wisdom, understanding, truth, and beauty come from completeness. A rounded approach to what is called self-development, including physical, mental, creative, scientific, and artistic qualities, was considered essential. However, the ideal of a coherent combination of one's various aspects has not been held up since the Renaissance.

Modern Western civilization is based on the supremacy of the mental body: Intellect rules over both spirit and emotion. But an overemphasis on the intellect inevitably robs the whole being of the powers of the united energy system.

Auguste Rodin's sculpture of The Thinker (*left*) *expresses the essence of human thought.*

mply put, the dominance of thought causes an nproductive build-up of issues in the emotional, piritual, and physical bodies, which leads to the evitable distortion of action in all spheres of the nergy body.

Sadly, those who are particularly intellectual ten have difficulty dealing with emotions or sponding easily to their physical side. And t, because Western society places such great alue on mental ability, people often give those with superior, usually highly trained, mental abilities a disproportionate influence over them. It is impossible to develop spirituality through intellect alone, though it can help enormously in spurring development. Also, because mental acuity demonstrates the ability to develop an area of energy significantly, it shows the capacity to develop all areas of energy in a similarly significant matter. One just needs to remember that intellect must be informed by emotion in order to empower personal and spiritual development.

This first-century mosaic depicts the school of Plato, whose teachings helped form much of Western philosophy.

THE EMOTIONAL BODY

Immediately surrounding the physical body is the energy band known as the emotional body. This is where emotions and their impact are held, felt, and exert their influence. The emotional body holds both the individual's emotional history and emotional capacity. In infants, the emotional body far outweighs the mental body, which is hardly developed at all.

Maintaining clear energy in the emotional body contributes to caring bevavior, which is essential to the world's survival.

As a baby feels, so he or she acts. As the infant grows to adulthood, nature and nurture interact in shaping thoughts, feelings, and behaviors. A well-developed and relatively clear emotional body indicates sensitivity to one's own emotions and to the feelings of others. This sensitivity partly results from having dealt with emotional areas that may have suffered from distortions. For example, repeated emotional pain may make an area inaccessible and thus cause particular blockages. Those kinds of marks remain throughout life. But, as one becomes more adept at dealing with and clearing the blockages or obstacles, they lose their power. The energy of the emotional body is able to expand and strengthen.

Unfortunately, the emotional arena, and so the emotional energy body, is easily confused and open to abuse. At the same time, interest in and emphasis on emotions have reached a level

precedented in history. Never before have
people had so much choice, and so little guidance,
this area.

Until the twentieth century duty, cultural custom,
family traditions, and personal responsibility had
always formed the framework within which
emotions were to be contained, although great
pain often resulted when emotions did not fit
within those clear expectations. But the breakdown
of those structures, and the explosion of economic
freedom, has changed all of that in the developed
world. Expectations, obligations, possibilities,
responsibilities, and choices are all contested.
At the same time, the emotional arena has been
stereotyped as "feminine," causing women to
be considered more emotionally involved and
articulate than men, with unfortunate
consequences for both sexes.

Meanwhile, many basic questions arise
about the ability to express emotions: Should
all feelings be experienced? Should some feelings
be suppressed, or indulged in? Are feelings to be
sought after or shunned? Are they to be analyzed,
exorcised, or even transcended? And if the
answer to any of the above is "yes," then how?

Without a firm moral and ethical framework—
ultimately a spiritual framework—to enable one
to identify desirable or appropriate feelings,
people have difficulty knowing how to handle
feelings or behaviors. For example, should one
look for pleasure above all else? Or is pleasure
to be treated with suspicion? Is one blocking
pleasure? Or is one flooding one's system with
inappropriate experiences? How does one deal
with childhood experiences? How does one
recognize emotional pain? And when should
one take it seriously? Are one's impressions
distorted by old pain? These kinds of questions
form the basis for problems and blockages in

Balancing the energy of the emotional body helps one
find productive ways to deal with feelings and desires.

one's emotional energy body. They are held,
along with the answers and the experiences in
trying to answer them, in one's emotional energy.

To successfully resolve emotional issues one
must work with the other subtle bodies too.
Because the energy of the emotional is slower than
the energy of the mental body, emotional energy
requires longer to take effect—a further
complication in balancing the mental and
emotional energy bodies. For example, a mental
decision about a relationship cannot be translated
into emotional reality immediately. One may
decide to end a relationship, but the feelings
involved take longer to resolve. Eventually, if one's
energy is in balance, both bodies come to hold
the same conclusion. Achieving balance in the
emotional, mental, and physical energy
bodies paves the way for
spiritual growth.

THE PHYSICAL BODY

The Chinese and Indian views of the way the human body works are based on the idea that energy moves as a kind of life force through the body. Both agree that the body's energy moves along unseen lines, known as "meridians," in the body. They also agree that certain sites on the body function like energetic fuse boxes, known as "chakras." The smooth functioning of these chakras is seen as crucial to well being.

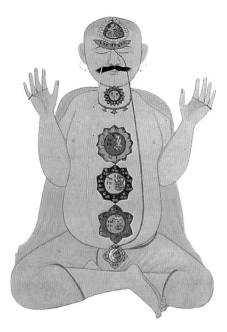

The seven chakras are represented in the pattern of flower petals in this ancient Hindu manuscript from Nepal, India.

Though the Chinese and Indian systems are slightly different, each forms the foundations of effective schools of medicine. At this time Western medicine and science have no place for energy and chakras, yet new developments are taking place that offer parallels to these ancient Eastern concepts. It is possible that conventional medicine may come to, or indeed may already be describing, the same underlying phenomena, but in the language of Western science, culture, and time.

This 19th century illustration in "Theosophica Practica" associates specific elements with each chakra.

Established medicine today incorporates certain ideas that are similar to aspects of the way chakras function. For example, just as each chakra is closely connected to some of the functions in the area around it, Western medicine recognizes that systems of organization based in specific areas are at work in the body. Recently, medical researchers have described a physical area surrounding the stomach as "the mini gut enteric brain," or a brain in the gut, which has its own sort of nervous system. This clearly parallels the third chakra, which also can be considered like a brain in the gut.

When it comes to the heart, various doctors have provided a number of arguments against considering it simply as a "dumb pump," ruled only by the brain's central system. Certain neurocardiologists describe the "little brain of the heart" and assign it both thinking and feeling functions. Strong comparisons can be made to the role of the heart chakra.

An exciting new breed of health care professionals is emerging, who call themselves medical intuitives, some of whom are trained doctors. They recognize and work with the chakras, relating physical ailments with them and with energy functioning. Yet intuitives, similar to the Indian and Chinese practitioners, differ slightly in their

interpretations. This may reflect differences in their individual qualities, or something else. Individuals who decide to explore this area further must trust their own judgment and intuition as a guide in assessing the information, always remembering that intuition develops and changes as one's maturity and understanding grows.

This medical illustration shows the Chinese acupuncture points that run along the meridian lines, which connect the seven main chakras.

Feeling energetic is a common experience for everyone. That sense is related to mechanical processes—eating and digesting, consuming and burning fuel. But that is far from the whole story. The energy within the body also is affected by that of the other energy bodies—and by the chakras, the body's energy junction boxes.

ENERGY WITHIN THE BODY

The chakras take in and distribute energy through the filter of the energy bodies. Having an idea of the role and function of each chakra is essential for using, and benefiting from, the meditation I teach. The meditation can address and change the energy at each chakra. In that way help deal with issues held in the chakra's energy. The clearer the chakra, the more effective it is. The more open the chakra, the wider the perspective it is able to incorporate.

The aim of the meditation I teach is to help one clear all the chakras and allow them to open as far as possible. This offers a way to deal with patterns in one's energy, caused by history or experience, and—crucially—of changing them. At the same time, the meditation also provides a route for widening and deepening one's outlook—a way to pursue physical, emotional, mental, and spiritual growth.

Clearing the chakras means that their structure is continually changing, both as one grows and as one's responses change. At times one particular

HE FELL

chakra is dominant, at others another, at still others, a mixture. As ever, individuals are multilayered, and the body's energy system reflects that fact.

The concept that each chakra holds information and history in the emotional, mental, and spiritual arenas has implications for physical well-being. However, some people take these ideas to extremes, believing that every problem that befalls them is due to unbalanced chakras.

Although events in the subtle energy bodies or chakras have an influence, they do not necessarily cause every illness that might affect one's body. The notion that one is totally responsible for any problem in the physical body is a punishing one. Many factors go into illness or injury, and not all of them are within one's control. But fortunately many are.

In addition to affecting physical well-being, chakras may influence an individual's ethical or moral values, and thereby social and collective life as well. Before exploring that, look more closely at the qualities and perspectives held at each chakra.

WHAT CHAKRAS DO

The body contains seven key chakras and many smaller ones. Each chakra relates in part to a particular area of the body, though it may not govern all functioning in that area. Each chakra also affects the body's overall functioning. In that way, chakras interact with the emotional, mental, and spiritual energy bodies.

Energy, meaning the subtle energy I am discussing here, travels through the spiritual, mental, and emotional subtle energy bodies and comes into the physical body through the chakras. The state of the subtle energy bodies affects how much, or what particular kind of, energy finds its way into the body. In the same way, the condition and functioning of the chakras play a key role in absorbing, modifying, and distributing energy.

Each chakra is especially attuned to particular frequencies. It has an influence in the area of the physical body around it, as well as in the balance of the whole. But chakras, like the arteries, can become blocked with old matter—"old energy"— that affects their functioning, particularly in the areas they directly influence. This energy usually concerns issues in the areas the chakra influences, which are not only physical (more on this later). The chakra's functioning relates to one's relationship and history with those issues.

The flow of energy through the chakras is particularly important because it transmits information, holds the memory of thought patterns and feelings, and thus the affect of history too. Because the chakras distribute energy, they also distribute thoughts, feelings, intentions, history, and more—the qualities of energy. Carrying all this, chakras can become blocked or even fail to open or only partially close. Clearing the paths for chakra functioning, along with the flow of the energy in the physical body, has implications for all of one's behaviors, thoughts, and feelings.

This 19th-century Thai manuscript depicts some of the "vital force" channels documented by ancient healters. They combine ancient Indian and Chinese health systems.

THE SEVEN KEY CHAKRAS

Connecting the body's seven key areas are lines of energy called meridians, which also contain many more, smaller chakras. Among the numerous minor chakras elsewhere on the body, those on the palms of the hands are particularly important for meditation. Exposing them by resting the palms positioned upwards allows more energy into the body.

The heart chakra relates to the chest area, between the breasts.

The crown chakra is associated with the area at the top of the head. High-quality energy can come through this chakra when it is open.

The third chakra is situated in the area of the navel.

The sixth chakra, located on the forehead, above the bridge of the nose.

The sexual chakra is located roughly halfway between the genitals and the navel.

The throat chakra, located at the throat.

The base chakra, located on the perineum, between the anus and the genitals.

A different color is associated with each of the main chakras. Remember the connection between color and energy? (See page 24.) With chakras, different systems suggest their own colors. I use a particular set of colors that came to me the first time I practiced meditation; others have developed different color associations for specific chakras. None of these color schemes are "wrong:" Various color associations are possible and those systems may be unique to each individual. The way the chakras fulfill their functions—that is, how they interact with each individual's history and development—is part of what defines one's energy.

THE ROLE OF THE BASE CHAKRA

The base chakra is the root of the body. I associate it with the color yellow. It represents the most basic family unit, which can be seen in various ways. In historical terms regarding the development of the human race, the base chakra is the smallest hunting or family group.

The base chakra's main concern is the immediate family. It represents infancy in human life.

In terms of each individual's life, the base chakra can represent infancy and all the issues of dependence associated with that and with growth throughout childhood, which is the process of progressing towards independence.

individuals whose base chakra is dominant are driven by concerns for their family's well being, at the expense of all else. They also can place a strong emphasis on their own needs and desires.

In positive terms, a strong family unit can be beneficial to its members and to the well-being of society as well, especially when the family becomes a coherent part of the larger whole. However, the emphasis on family can also result in self-interest, or family interest, outweighing other aims, from the desire for harmonious personal relations with others outside the family to the well-being of the overall community.

As far as the physical body is concerned, different medical intuitives make slightly different associations. Although I am not a medical intuitive, I see the base chakra

as having particularly strong connections with the feet, legs, buttocks (including the anus and the process of eliminating waste from the body), and hips. Injury to any of these parts affects and reflects damage at the base chakra.

A well-functioning base chakra is essential to stability and the ability to develop into a fully contributing adult.

POSITION OF THE BASE CHAKRA

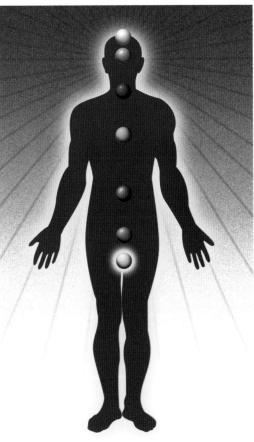

The base chakra has strong connections with the feet, legs, buttocks (including the elimination process), and hips.

THE ROLE OF THE SEXUAL CHAKRA

I see the sexual chakra as a medium blue color. At the sexual (or second) chakra, the individual associates with a larger social unit, rather than just the small family group. At this phase, the relevant group is a club or an even larger unit, but still one held together by self-interest. Think of the early teenage years and the gang mentality, or athletic clubs, or even political parties.

The teenage years, especially early on, provide a good metaphor for this chakra generally, because that is also the time of life when puberty strikes. (As the onset of puberty appears at ever-earlier ages, more pressure appears on both the base and this chakra.)

Obviously, this center also is concerned with sexual issues, in particular the "sex drive" and the physical aspects of sexual relations. The sexual chakra also is associated with reproduction, although it does not have full responsibility for every aspect of the expression of sexual relations.

Just as the desire for sexual fulfilment can be a motivating force, so can the need for money and for food. For that reason, many physical, emotional, and social issues

The sexual chakra affects an individual's views and reactions toward physical relationships with others.

Naturally, a healthy sexual chakra is essential for well-being, including sexual responses, reproduction, a balanced sense of self, and the ability to earn a living. The second chakra exerts a great deal of influence in our society, particularly today. Unlike the first chakra, the second chakra identifies one with a larger group. This link is what causes polarization and the equivalent of "gang warfare." Even when disguised in "civilized" adult terms, fighting can be dirty at the second chakra and people can become blinded by loyalty to a chosen group.

This chakra is associated with the teen years, when people tend to identify themselves in terms of their social group—a main theme in the classic '50s film, West Side Story.

...lating to consumption and moderating it are governed by the sexual chakra. Thus, issues that deal with food and money, as well as addiction issues, are often influenced by the sexual chakra too.

A blockage at the second chakra, or obstructions in that area, may result from difficulties in or after puberty, problems related to sexual development (including sexual abuse), a sense of being fruitful or barren, feelings of power or impotence in the world, fears of poverty or hunger, greed, or other issues. If the energy blockage or obstructions in this area actually enter the physical body, the sort of problems that can appear include diseases of the reproductive or sexual organs, bladder, and urinary tract, eating disorders, problems with sexual potency, alcohol or other substance addictions, and problems with the lower back (which is often associated with finances).

POSITION OF THE SEXUAL CHAKRA

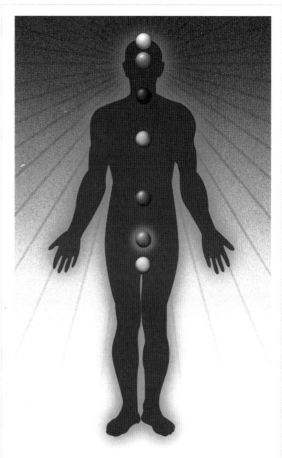

The sexual chakra influences issues relating to sexuality, reproduction, self-esteem, and earning a living.

THE ROLE OF THE THIRD CHAKRA

I see the third chakra as red. A surprising color, perhaps, to be especially involved with knowledge and its implications: "Gut knowledge." In individual terms, the chakra corresponds to the onset of adulthood, when it becomes particularly important to "know," or to be seen to know, because knowledge represents power and authority.

Red is a color of power. Because being seen or considered to "know" is important, the adult at the third chakra feels the influence of a wider strategic group, perhaps even a nation. The individual is able, or wants, to identify with a group at this level. At the same time, perhaps under the influence of self-importance—or its opposite, sense of inferiority—the hold of the emotions can be very strong here. The adult needs to feel secure in his or her knowledge, and so must believe he or she is right. This urge can give rise to strongly held views, with the power to act on them. Or, in some cases, individuals feel so insecure about their beliefs that they argue more vehemently than necessary.

Physically, the third chakra involves the stomach, internal organs (such as the pancreas,

The third chakra is linked to one's responses to "adult" situations, such as committee meetings or office politics.

then may be strongly acted upon, with adult force. If the blockages in the energy reach the physical body, disease or injury can follow. But disease also is influenced by several other factors, from genetic makeup to food intake. A well-functioning third chakra, as with other chakras, may help provide protection against other influences, such as genetic tendencies.

spleen, kidneys, liver, and gallbladder), and the intestines. Digestion issues, often linked to intellectual and emotional issues, all play their part here. Issues around what a person perceives as taking on adult power—whatever that may be—make themselves known.

On the positive side, a well-functioning third chakra brings the ability to deal with ideas and feelings effectively, and to hold an adult position in society. When obstructions occur in the third chakra, they can lead to ideas or feelings being badly digested or processed. They

POSITION OF THE THIRD CHAKRA

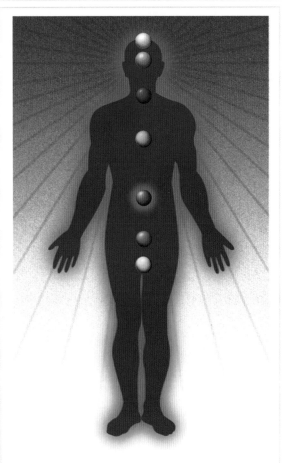

The third chakra affects the stomach, internal organs (such as the pancreas, spleen, liver, kidneys, and gallbladder), and intestines.

THE ROLE OF THE HEART CHAKRA

I see the heart chakra as green. It is located in the center of the chest, between the breasts. The heart chakra symbolizes maturity. Though expressions like "straight from the heart" are commonplace, developing the energy of the heart is a lifetime's work, and can only be fully achieved if the chakras below the heart have been addressed.

The heart's energy reveals that a true, mature understanding and use of power is different from the simple enforcement of authority. The heart is about love, a love that knows no boundaries and has achieved wisdom, free from the fight or flight response Unlike the previous three chakras, all of which use or explore their power with particular reference to an interest group of some sort—the family, the social circle, or even the nation—the heart chakra provides the true understanding that people are interconnected The heart knows that no one person, or one group, can truly benefit at the expense of another.

In contrast, this knowledge has hardly begun to dawn at the lower three chakras. For example, at the sexual chakra, the individual feels the need to exert him- or herself to achieve supremacy over someone else, and also has a great desire for his or her "gang" to win. But once the power of the heart has developed, one becomes aware that all people are interdependent.

The heart's realization makes it impossible to consider individual well-being except as part of the whole—a fact that business and economic communities are beginning to take seriously. Thinkers at the forefront of many corporations realize it is not possible to avoid being affected by the economies of other countries. For example, economic collapse in Asia in 1997 and 1998 quickly fed through to the rest of the world. There are, to use the technical term, no "firewalls" in the world's economic reality anymore. This is just one area where people are learning the lessons of the heart for the survival of the universe.

The heart chakra is also about personal relationships. Union or partnership is no longer concerned with issues of individuality. At the second chakra, even in sexual union, power struggles abound about remaining separate or merging in some way. At the heart chakra, no power struggle or desire to control the other is necessary. At the heart, the aim is harmony and becoming one in a way that fully acknowledges that there is no true gain at the other's expense.

This ability of the heart to embrace unity brings another gift: Intuition. Living from the heart chakra strengthens and builds intuition in a way that can only contribute to the good, because it has the welfare of the other at its heart and recognizes the unity of self and the other. At its base, well-founded intuition about others stems from the ability to put oneself in another's shoes and to know life as the other does.

Intuition about oneself, as well as events in the world, is seen as increasingly desirable today. The best way to develop one's intuition is to develop one's heart. While intuition can be a wonderful and natural gift, it can also be a powerful and potentially dangerous tool.

It can be developed and used for dubious purposes, often based in the desire to exert power over others. But intuition that flows from developing the heart is utterly benevolent. It cannot be other than that.

Finally, only the heart is capable of giving and receiving the quality of love that is essential to the survival of the human race and the planet. Entering the domain of the heart chakra is an immense privilege and responsibility for all.

POSITION OF THE HEART CHAKRA

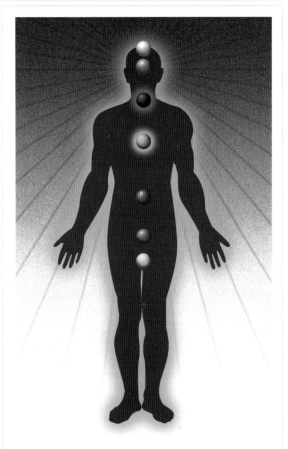

Physical problems associated with the heart chakra often concern the heart itself or the breasts. Giving too much away or receiving hostility, especially in intimate relationships, may cause problems.

The heart involves one's relationship to the larger world, as well as to individual loved ones.

THE ROLE OF THE THROAT CHAKRA

The upper chakras, beyond the heart, have ethical systems of their own, and no automatic constituencies. They take the values of the most developed, dominant chakra below, whether it is the heart or another. The throat chakra, which I see as dark blue, has a special connection with the second chakra, which is medium blue.

Like the second chakra, the throat chakra, which includes the mouth, has a role in consumption. Food to nourish the body is taken in through the mouth and then passes down the throat. Both the mouth and throat are governed by the throat chakra.

Physically the throat area is vulnerable to a variety of ailments connected with communication or self-expression. For example, a stiff neck can reflect rigidly held ideas. A sore throat, tonsillitis, or strep throat may suggest that a person feels unable to speak out about what he or she sees, feels, or understands. (This condition is often found in children who do not feel able to express their perceptions or feelings.) A sore or hoarse throat may relate to not speaking the truth.

The throat chakra is linked with isssues of eating and self expression. Both involve the mouth and throat.

ngers' throats are particularly vulnerable because
ey are so conscious of the role of the throat in
.pressing themselves, and so attentive to the
uality of the sound their throats make.

Eating habits also reflect blockages in the energy
the throat chakra. A person who has difficulty
pressing him- or herself may develop eating
oblems, such as anorexia or compulsive eating
hich are often also connected with sexual issues
overned by the second chakra).

The throat chakra is unique because it has
"a voice." The energy at the throat finds expression
through the individual's voice. When listening to
the qualities of the voice, one can become sensitive
to the energy of the throat, which reflects the
qualities of the chakra syatem. In this way the
throat chakra conveys a great deal of information
about the individual.

Singers are especially
aware of the sound and
affect of the voice, which
is connected to the throat
chakra. Edward Barhum
dramatically portrays
emotions in Don Carlos.

POSITION OF THE THROAT CHAKRA

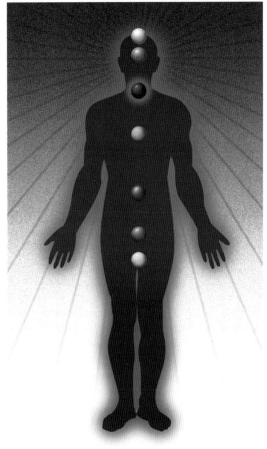

The mouth, throat,and neck are associated with the
throat chakra. Eating disorders may reflect issues
pertaining to the throat chakra and second chakra.

THE ROLE OF THE SIXTH CHAKRA

I see the sixth chakra as orange. Physically, the sixth chakra includes the nose, eyes, ears, and brain—all the organs of perception. It is associated with the ancient Eastern concept of the "third eye," which often is regarded as a magic eye with the special ability of second sight.

The witches in Shakespeare's Macbeth *show the danger that may come when humans deal with dark forces.*

Like the throat chakra, the sixth chakra does not relate to a particular societal system. Rather, it reflects the dominant chakra below, which depends on the individual. If the heart is the dominant chakra below, the perceptual abilities of the third eye are at the heart's service. If, on the other hand, the third chakra is the strongest chakra below, the sixth chakra perceives the matter from a more "adult" or authoritarian point of view.

The third eye is thought to bestow "second sight," such as clairvoyance and intuition. Although this is true and there are ways of developing these perceptual abilities, these efforts work only to a limited extent. They actually develop in a much wiser, stronger way, naturally, along with the development

When left to evolve naturally, the "third eye" chakra offers enlightening input into the normal process of individual integration and evolution, bringing greater sensitivity and awareness. In some cases, as the "third eye" chakra opens or clears, the abilities of intuition, including clairvoyance, become more pronounced. (However, in these cases, the experiences are never sought.) For those who have truly opened their hearts, the direction that develops at the sixth chakra is of no consequence. These individuals simply want to use their gifts appropriately, to the best of their ability and for the benefit of all.

POSITION OF THE SIXTH CHAKRA

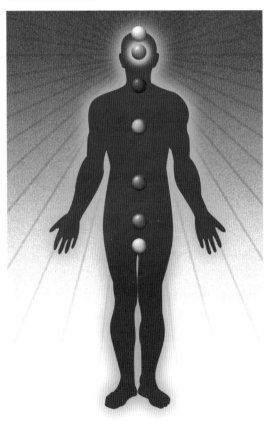

The sixth chakra is affiliated with all the organs of perception—the nose, eyes, ears, and brain.

f the heart chakra. The more open one's heart, ne easier one finds it to understand others, and nerefore to accept, forgive, and embrace them. 'hen this development is part of the evolution f the human heart, then intuitive abilities develop aturally, within a spiritual framework. They are easy o experience and accept as part of a normal life, so nat one sees and feels that they are appropriate.

When intuitive abilities are unnaturally sought fter and developed in an accelerated manner, they an grow outside a spiritual framework in unnatural r unethical ways. This could leave the seeker aumatized by frightening experiences, such s witchcraft, gripped by desire for power over thers, or vulnerable to being controlled by others.

THE ROLE OF THE CROWN CHAKRA

At the top of the head is

a wonderful chakra, called

the "crown chakra," which

literally crowns the body.

This chakra is most closely

associated with the finest

energy, allowing only the

purest, most spiritual input

into the body.

Again, like the throat and sixth chakras, the crown is influenced by the dominant chakra or chakras below. This plays a part in controlling exactly how much energy is absorbed at the crown, how it is used, and how it is perceived, or understood, by the individual.

An open crown chakra is a blessing. If all the chakras are functioning well and entrained to the heart, the crown is wide open. An open crown chakra without the stabilizing and developing influences of the lower chakras can lead to what I sometimes call the "the joy bunny" approach: ungrounded behavior and unrealistic attitudes that can cause one to lose touch with reality. But supported by and supporting of the whole system, the crown chakra offers the ultimate joy.

Above the crown chakra is another, rarely spoken of, chakra. The eighth chakra, directly above the body, exerts great power in linking the body with the higher dimensions. It involves a type of energy that perhaps cannot be absorbed in everyday life. The eighth chakra cannot be cultivated by choice or effort, and only appears when all the centers below it are already functioning well. Physically, the eighth chakra does not have great significance, as it is not concerned with the issues of individual life on earth. Its appearance may, however, indicate the onset of death, or the ability to live in the face of death. All of these chakras, except the eighth, can be influenced by the meditation that I teach. When the eighth chakra opens, the chakra meditation itself points to the next way of moving forward.

CHAKRA DISCOVERY

In my case, I discovered the eighth chakra after working through the chakra meditation to the crown. At the crown chakra, another chakra waited, one that I had no idea existed.

This eighth chakra produced the impetus for a different kind of meditation that followed. This meditation took me on a further journey; for me, the major journey.

Years later, as I continue to teach others, I have yet to encounter anyone who has worked with the eighth chakra. However, at the time it appeared to me, I was, unknowingly, close to death. Perhaps then, this further journey is one that only those close to death, or otherwise marked, travel. Meanwhile, over the years, I have had the privilege of working with many others in long and rich journeys through the chakras to the glory of the crown.

POSITION OF THE CROWN CHAKRA

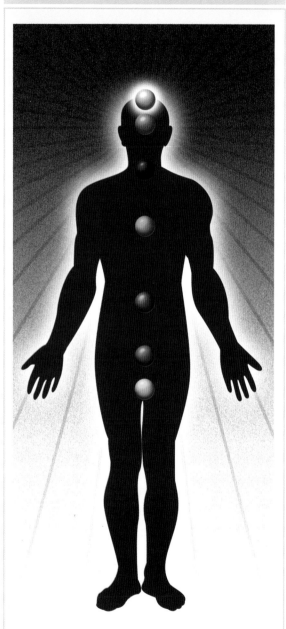

THE CROWN CHAKRA is influenced by the dominant chakra or chakras below, which affects the quality and amount of energy absorbed through the crown chakra and how it is used.

MEDITATION

Words are easy, relatively speaking. But words that produce no result are lost. Words need to have an effect on behavior. Ultimately it is actions that count. Actions are a way of proving words. Actions are a way of testing the reality that the words uphold. It is time to try meditation.

Practice is an adventure. A refuge.

A pleasure. A statement of intention.

It is a means of making clear to oneself,

not just by words, but by deeds, one's

aspirations. It is also a way of taking

practical steps toward change.

PREPARING TO MEDITATE

I first approached meditation in desperation, but also with no expectations. I despaired of ever finding a way to deal with whatever it was that was clawing at me. But, more than anything, I wanted to understand. At the same time I certainly didn't hold out much hope that meditation would offer any answers. Of course, it was precisely that combination that showed me the door, and unlocked it.

In approaching meditation, it is important not to hold on to expectations. They block the process. I do not teach a way to fantastic out-of-this-world experiences, the weird and the wonderful. All I teach is a way within.

Ultimately, if true desire and intention are strong enough, the way within will open. It is

INTO THE DEEPER DOMAIN
*A picture created during the period
I was spending much time in intense meditation.*

a way that connects with a larger whole—whatever name, or names, one puts to that reality. The word that to me is simplest and best, is God. Not God as some external power, an old man in the sky ordering heaven and hell at a whim or according to a secret plan. But the spiritual dimension of each person, which transcends the petty—but hugely important—human reality, and connects in the reality of a supreme force. A force which is larger than the sum of all one's combined parts, and truly Divine in the scope of its understanding and power to influence reality. It makes all individuals intimately connected, altogether responsible, and equally able to own God and power.

THE ENVIRONMENT

The place where one chooses to practice meditation, the time of day and surroundings are all important. Each affects progress in subtle ways. Domestic responsibilities do not promote tranquillity, whatever the time of day. At the same time, given the choice, some times of day are better than others.

TIME OF DAY

There are many theories about the rhythms of the body, from ayurverdic ideas that there are fixed cycles to the day, to notions relating peak activity periods to birthtime, to some views of traditional Chinese acupuncture wherein different organs function optimally at different times. Generally though, the body is more receptive to meditation early in the morning and in the evening.

In energetic and environmental terms, there is usually less disturbance in the early morning, before the bustle of the day begins, or in the evening, when events have settled down. The atmosphere is calmer and therefore conducive to a practice requiring openness and sensitivity to subtle influences. As anyone who has walked in the dawn, or lingered at dusk knows. Consequently, if possible, choose one, or both, of those times if it can be maintained, and does not conflict with other responsibilities. Establishing a rhythm is helpful, including meditating regularly at around the same time on each occasion.

PLACE

Privacy matters. So choose surroundings that feel comfortable, taking into account all the factors described in The Energy of Objects & Places on page 22.

WOODEN CHAIR

The chair used during meditation is important. I do not recommend sitting cross-legged on the floor. Most Westerners who are not accustomed to sitting in this way are rather uncomfortable doing so—at least for a while. On the whole, I find sitting on a chair, with the feet flat on the ground more satisfactory. But the construction and material the chair is significant. Wood is best because absorbs fear and helps to ground energy. Above l, the chair must be stable, with four legs well alanced on the floor.

GHT A CANDLE

tention, as ever, is crucial. To signify the intention, m, and desire to reach towards the Divine, or ivine realms, light a candle. The candle is a mbol of the light of spirituality. In my own ractice, I often use not one but three candles. he number three has a special significance in any traditions. It is the Holy Trinity in the hristian tradition. It also stands for the mind, ody, and soul of modern seekers. In the Buddhist adition, it is the Triple Jewel, the archetypal vocation. In numerological theory, it can idicate the fruitful union. For me, it has particular significance. The first time I aw a client—when I did not believe

the session would reveal anything at all, but had reluctantly agreed to offer it—almost automatically, I lit three candles. When my client asked why I lit three, I opened my mouth to say it was only a whim. Instead, I found a stream of words emerging that explained some of what I say here, and more!

FREQUENCY

It is a matter of choice whether one meditates as much as twice daily, or as infrequently as once a week. However, less than twice a week makes the effort much slower to be felt. At the same time, there is no virtue or positive effect (indeed, it may be counterproductive) in meditating for what seems "a long time." The practice should last exactly as long as feels comfortable, whether that is five or twenty-five minutes.

PRAYER

Prayer is an integral part of meditation. Like everything else, prayer is energy. It is like a special energetic message. People who pray regularly know its power, they know that it works. Not as mere wish fulfillment, but as a means of connecting with a much deeper layer of meaning and causality in the Universe. One that recognizes the existence of a greater whole that surrounds us, influences us, and of which we are a part.

This group of men, wearing traditional Turkish hats and dress, kneel when joining together in prayer.

The clergy or religious groups almost never succumb to scientific experiments to test the power of prayer—it is rather like testing God. But in his book *Reinventing Medicine*, Larry Dossey, MD, includes an example of a clergyman who set up an experiment to test the power of prayer. Father Sean O'Laoire, a Catholic priest and psychologist working in the San Francisco bay area, presented a paper at a Harvard University Conference in 1997 on distant healing. He studied the effects of prayer on 406 distressed people, half of whom received prayer and half of whom did not. O'Laoire found that those prayed for improved in all eleven of the criteria he used to measure self esteem, anxiety, and depression. However, he also discovered that the agents doing the prayer improved more than the subjects for whom they were praying for ten of his eleven criteria!

*a temple in Ranchi,
dia, this Buddhist
onk recites prayers,
nctuating them with
e beat of a drum.*

f course, this was a
mall study and the
ethodology is open
 investigation, but
e findings
e intriguing.
Findings like these
esonate not only
ith the experiences of those
ho pray, but with discoveries
 modern physics. For example,
on-Locality Theory, firmly established in
odern physics, suggests that no matter where
ne is in the world, what happens around him
r her is affected immediately by events all over
e universe. In other words the whole universe
 interconnected. In the words of the poet John
onne, "No man is an island." The thoughts,
tentions, and actions of one directly affect the
ell-being of another, or all others. It suggests
at one day science will establish a basis
r the power of prayer and distant healing.
 also believe each individual has the potential
 be more, to be greater. This knowledge is
arried in the heart. One way of describing this
rocess of becoming greater is as connecting
ith or enabling a greater whole within, at the
ame time as connecting with the greater whole
ithout—which is the entire universe. Prayer can
lay a key role in the process. It acknowledges
eing part of a greater whole. It is also an

acknowledgement of
the influence of a greater whole.
And, crucially, it is a statement of the desire
to be whole, to be greater, and to be connected
with a greater whole. At the same time, the
energetic effects of sound and thought—hearing
the words and thinking the thoughts—all make
their contribution to the process. That is why
those who pray know the power of prayer. There
are no right or wrong prayers. No rules about
prayer. Authenticity is all. Prayer is simple.

*Beware of the scribes, which love to go in long clothing,
and love salutations in the market places,
And the chief seats in the synagogues, and the
uppermost rooms in feasts:
Which devours widows houses, and for pretense
Makes long prayers.*

—Mark 12:18

SIMPLE PRAYERS

The most effective prayer is the prayer that comes from the heart. There are no special formulations to remember, or books to research. The lips give expression to the heart. Sometimes I use the word God. It is a shorthand I am comfortable with. But, it does not indicate a deity in the sky, or some overwhelming authority figure. Nor is it preferable to any of a myriad expressions. "The Light," "the Creative," and many more are equally relevant.

Here are a few prayers that I have used. They are very simple.

JELALUDDIN RUMI

SUFI MYSTIC, 13TH CENTURY

O love, O pure deep love, be here, be now.
Be all; worlds dissolve into your stainless endless radiance,
Frail living leaves burn with you brighter than cold starts;
Make me your servant, your breath, your core.

❖

SIMPLE PRAYER

Dear God,
Bless us. Keep us. Help us. Teach us Love.
Teach us to love one another, to love you,
and above all to love ourselves as you,
and as you would.
Thank you God.
Amen

❖

BUDDHIST PRAYER

REPEATED AFTER MEDITATION

By the power and truth of this practice,
May all beings have happiness
and the causes of happiness,
May all beings be free from sorrow
and the causes of sorrow,
May all never be separated from the
sacred happiness which is sorrowless,
And may all live within equanimity,
Without too much attachment
and too much aversion,
And live believing in the
equality of all that lives.

NORTH AMERICAN INDIAN—CHINOOK

May all I say and all I think
be in harmony with Thee,
God within me, God beyond me,
Maker of the Trees.
Amen.

UNIVERSAL PRAYER

Show me the stars in the sky, and the sun in the mist,
and the world beyond the world of the everyday.
Teach me tolerance, wisdom and, always, love.
Thank you God,
Amen

JULIAN OF NORWICH

(BORN C. 1342)

God of your goodness, give me yourself; for you are
sufficient for me. I cannot properly ask anything less, to
be worthy of you. If I were to ask less, I should always be
in want. In you alone do I have all.

THE PEACE PRAYER

BASED ON AN OLD HINDU PRAYER

Lead me from death to life, from falsehood to truth,
Lead me from despair to hope, from fear to trust,
Lead me from hate to love, from war to peace.
Let peace fill our hearts, our world, our universe,
Peace, peace, peace.

WILLIAM PENN

(QUAKER, 1644-1714)

Oh Lord, help me not to despise or oppose what
I do not understand.

LOVE

To the Power of the Universe, to the Creative,
to the God in me, to the God in the world,
to the God in us all—be with me.
Love me, let me love, and being loved,
be you, be love.
Amen.

SECRET WISDOM

Lord,
Teach us the wisdom of the seasons,
and the secret of night and day.
Teach us the meaning of the clouds
and the feelings of the waves.
Teach us the power of the wind,
and the silence of the mountains.
Teach us stillness and action, love, laughter,
pain and despair. Then teach us stillness again.
Teach us to find you and ourselves.
Thank you.
Amen.

SARUM PRIMER PRAYER

(C. 1514)

God be in my head
And in my understanding;
God be in my eyes and in my looking;
God be in my mouth and in my speaking;
God be in my heart
And in my thinking;
God be at my end and in my departing.
Peace, peace, peace.

The background images on these pages come from a
photograph of strings of colorful Buddhist prayer flags.

ALIGNMENT OF THE BODY

The old saying "Cleanliness

is next to Godliness" is true

in approaching meditation.

Wash, if possible, avoid

perfume, aftershave, or

traces of any strong scent.

Sit on a wooden chair, in

a chosen place, beside a

lighted candle, say a prayer,

and think about the body.

Sitting straight is important. The way the body is held can help the energy flow smoothly through a the channels, or it can emphasise obstacles and further blocks. There are a number of key points.

First is the position of the spine, which will probably change as the practice deepens. In the beginning, it is particularly important to hold the back as straight as possible because the energy travels up the spine. However, holding the back in too rigid a position may cause problems, just as allowing it to slouch may.

The position of the spine often changes as the meditation practice develops. Sometimes phases occur when the back does not seem comfortable, or the body is racked by involuntary energy bumps or jerks. These are simply evidence of energy flowing through new or unaccustomed channels. It is proof of the rearrangement of the body's energy as the meditation practice helps to purify and expand it.

Sometimes, physical manipulation, from an osteopath, chiropractor, or Alexander teacher, for example, can be really helpful in assisting the back to find a comfortable position. But allowing too much input from a body worker can interfere with allowing this process to settle organically as the body finds its truest position.

In sitting, give thought to the center line. This is an imaginary line that runs through the body, from the crown to the base. It symbolizes the development of the body from the first bundle

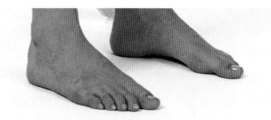

The hands can rest with the palms down, or cupped with the backs of the hands on the thighs.

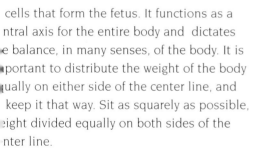

ding the back as straight as possible, without being id, enables energy to flow smoothly along the spine.

The feet should always be positioned flat on the ground, preferably barefoot, to remain grounded to the "earth."

cells that form the fetus. It functions as a ntral axis for the entire body and dictates e balance, in many senses, of the body. It is portant to distribute the weight of the body ually on either side of the center line, and keep it that way. Sit as squarely as possible, eight divided equally on both sides of the nter line.

Emphasizing one side of the body or the her may indicate an emphasis on what can thought of as the male or the female alities. Leaning to the right often suggests tting more weight on male characteristics, ligations, or duties. Leaning to the left, puts eight on those that can be characterized as male. (This left/right alignment is not a iversal law though; in some cases it is versed.) If the center line seems to be out place, try visualizing it in the proper place encourage the appropriate development.

The position of the hands and feet is also crucial. The usual position for the hands is either at rest on the thighs, palms down, or held cupped with the backs of the hands resting on the thighs. Because of the chakras that exist on the palms of the hands, exposing the palms can increase the energy taken into the body, and so, potentially, speed up the meditation process. Placing the palms face down on the thighs can lead to a slower, steadier pace in meditation practice.

The feet have only one position: Flat on the ground. The soles of the feet need to be in contact with the "earth," or the floor, at all times. It helps to take one's shoes off, to leave the vibrations they collect behind, and to allow the feet direct contact with the ground.

Before starting the chakra meditation, which is the main meditation practice, I recommend a preparatory practice, which is a visualization. Next, I explain how that works.

ABOUT VISUALIZATION

Visualization works by suggesting a series of images and describing their results. In some cases, it works by suggesting the image or images and leaving the subject to experience their effects spontaneously. In this way, visualization uses the ability of the body to respond automatically to images in order to produce a parallel effect on its energy.

Just as many athletes condition their bodies to move with efficiency and strength, they direct thoughts towards a positi outlook, and a rehearsal of winning, through visualization.

For example, a person with a phobia about snake responds with fear or anxiety to a picture of a snake. In another example, looking at a picture a lemon can elicit a change in saliva secretions. Conversely, positive images can introduce positiv or stimulating effects. For more than twenty years medicine has been working with some of the implications of this ability of visual imagery to rectly affect physiology. In particular, alternative approaches to cancer treatment use a wide range of visualization techniques to alleviate symptoms and promote healing. Although there is much debate on how far visualization actually affects outcome in terms of life expectancy for cancer sufferers, in many cases, it clearly seems to help people deal with some of the symptoms produced by the disease.

Visualization is not about wish fulfilment. Spending half an hour a day visualizing oneself on vacation on a tropical island does not mean the airplane tickets magically appear in the mail. But it can deliver some of the physical and mental advantages of taking that vacation. At the same time, the images are like metaphors. Sometimes they may seem simple, even crude. However, they are not significant in themselves. Their significance lies in what they stand for, and the effects they produce. Using the images is like using a map. They are no substitute for the journey – but they can provide a guide for the journey.

The visualization that follows is very specific: it promotes the state of being grounded. That is the quality of being rooted in the everyday, of being able to deal easily and naturally with all the events that arise in the everyday. Walking barefoot on a beach, or feeling the grass between one's toes, often makes life seem simple; events are easy to deal with. That is the experience of being well grounded. In an office building bombarded by computer rays and a huge diversity of energies, matters are quite different. It can be difficult to deal with the everyday. It becomes harder to be realistic or to live up to ideals, however sincerely they are held. All these problems are typical of an "ungrounded" approach. To be able to assess reality effectively, to hold and to implement ideas appropriately, requires a well-grounded approach.

This visualization is a preparatory practice for the chakra meditation, which can produce powerful results. To get the most benefit from the potential results, one must be well grounded. Of course, in practical terms, seeing oneself as grounded does not automatically produce that effect. But it is part of producing that effect, just as an athlete, intent on winning a race, uses the technique of visualizing him- or herself winning. It is not simply wish fulfilment, nor is it effective unless it is part of an overall strategy. Properly understood and used, visualization plays a valuable part in producing the desired effect.

PROCEED WITH CARE

The chakra meditation that follows is simple. But, as with much that is simple, its potential and implications are profound. I recommend having no expectations of the process, rather than hoping for vast results. In the beginning, and possibly for years, judging the results is almost impossible, which is just as well.

To be effective, the chakra meditation needs to become a habit. Once a day at the same time of day, if possible, – or even twice a day – is probably best. It can be limited to as seldom as twice a week, however, at that point the benefits of the exercise diminish.

A final word of caution. These instructions are precise. I advise against improvising when following this meditation. Unless one has a prior, in-depth understanding of energetic development, I recommend closely following the instructions for this meditation in order to achieve results.

THE VISUALIZATION

Understanding energy and feeling firmly rooted prepare the way for the chakra meditation that follows. This visualization helps develop the feeling of being grounded or rooted

Sitting comfortably on a wooden chair, feet flat on the ground, candle alight nearby, close the eyes and say a prayer.

Then allow the following sequence to unfold.

A pleasant field on a summer's day is the setting for the first image of this visualization.

Concentrate your attention on your feet. Your feet are resting on the earth. The rich earth. The soil is soft but firm beneath your feet. There is a slight just perceptible sense of heat filtering through the soles of your feet from the ground. It is a warm day. Pleasantly warm, not too hot. The sky is still. The gentle sounds around you blend into one another. Your attention is on your feet. They are growing warmer now.

Watch, as slowly, it seems, first one, then another, then an entire delicate network of roots emerge—tentatively at first—from the soles of your feet and slip down into the earth. They are growing stronger and surer now. They push their way through the compacted soil and anchor your

et firmly to the ground. You are rooted. Like a
lant you are rooted in the soil. Through your
oots you draw nourishment and sustenance, the
oodness of the earth.

The roots spread in a complicated, complex
attern. Then a new development begins. As
ou watch, rooted to the spot, a small round
hape starts to form on one of the roots beneath
our feet. Quickly it is joined by others. Together
hey grow, holding to the roots, clusters of firm
ound shapes, swelling as the roots bring
ourishment from the rich earth to them.

Soon there is a huge and intricate network
eneath your feet. Your roots spread deep into
e ground below you. Dotted everywhere along
ose roots are rich stores of nutrients, held in

rounded shapes, like potatoes, or elongated,
like carrots, or simply swollen, as tubers, holding
the goodness of the earth. And they hold this
goodness, this energy from the earth, for you. It
is your reserves, your store to use when you need.
Not only are you rooted to the earth, but you are
provided for from the earth too. Hold this reality.
Know this knowledge that flows from the soles
of your feet. As you acknowledge it, it is yours.

When you are ready, open your eyes, taking
with you the world beneath your feet.

Here lands female and male,

Here the heir-ship and heiress-ship of the world,

here the flame of materials,

Here Spirituality, the translatress,

the openly-avowed,

The ever-tending, the finale of visible forms,

The satisfier, after due long-waiting, now advancing,

Yes, here comes the mistress, The Soul.

The SOUL!

Forever and forever—longer than soil is brown

and solid—longer than water ebbs and flows.

I will make the poems of materials,

for I think they are to be the most spiritual of poems,

And I will make the poems of my body and of mortality,

For I think I shall then supply myself with the

poems of my Soul and of immortality.

—Walt Whitman, from "Leaves of Grass" (1860)

THE MEDITATION

In "Leaves of Grass," Walt Whitman deals with the eternal forces. First the male and the female. Next the material. Then spirituality, "the translatress," the bridge between the material and what he calls "the mistress"— the Soul. "The satisfier after due long-waiting." There are many ways of describing the development of the human. Many ways too of describing the progression from the material world to the non-material, as well as the relationship between the two. Or even the understanding that transcends the duality between the two. But one point Whitman understands and makes so well is that the process is a material one.

In describing the progression of spirituality he writes, "I will make these poems of materials, for I think they are to be the most spiritual of poems, And I will make the poems of myself, And I will make the poems of my body and of mortality,

For I think I shall then supply myself with the poems of my Soul and of immortality."

In other words, in the quest for what Whitman calls "The Soul," the understanding known to each by so many different names, it is necessary to work with the material. To use the material substances that are at hand. In Whitman's case, the material means are words shaped into poetry to describe that which transcends words. Here, the tool is meditation. It is a process that may seem clumsy, even ill suited to its purpose. The words used to describe the process may seem unworthy. Or the aspirant's efforts, apparently inconsequential. None of this is true. As Whitman illustrates so beautifully, to make the poems of immortality one must use the body and mere material means. Meditation is a material means to transcend the merely material.

AS ABOVE SO BELOW

This picture represents the correspondence between the layers of the universe—as above, so below.

CHAKRA MEDITATION

After mastering the visualization, the chakra meditation follows. The purpose of this meditation is to gain access to the chakras, and thereby the body's energy. This helps with releasing the elements of personal history that have settled in the form of obstacles, marks, or blockages in one's energy. With this release, the implications for health and well-being are profound. Change becomes inevitable.

1. ENTERING THE MEDITATION

Prepare in the customary way: Sit in a calm place, on a wooden chair, in an upright, comfortable position. Light a candle…or three. Say a prayer. Then…

FOCUS THE MIND on the base chakra. That is, focus on the area of the perineum, which is between the genitals and the anus. Continue to concentrate on the base chakra, then mentally switch it "on." This is a way of gaining access to the base chakra. It can work by simply visualizing the chakra lit up, and therefore "on." Or try using a device. For example, imagine a light switch, and then push it to the "on" position. When it clicks "on," I see the color yellow (although there is no one, correct color). If another color appears instead of yellow, it may indicate that an individual's mind is aligned with a different color system, which can reflect aspects of that individual's heritage, abilities, experience, or something else.

GUARD AGAINST DOUBT at this stage. Lighting the chakra may take several attempts. Questioning whether or not the chakra is "on," or shows the "proper" color, invariably causes problems. It can prevent one seeing any sign of color or light. However, trusting that color and light do eventually come makes it easier for exactly that to happen.

MOVE THE LIGHT, once the chakra is alight, up the body, to the center of the forehead. Or picture an image of the body, then watch the light move up in it. When the light reaches the forehead, stop.

HOLD THE LIGHT outside the body, and focus on it. Avoid focussing with the eyes. Concentrate on the yellow light from a point in the center of the forehead.

ALLOW WHATEVER THOUGHTS come to mind to do so. Control has no place. If one's thoughts wander to the laundry or some equally mundane task, allow that. If a past or future event comes to mind, allow that too. At all times, allow the movement of thoughts to be fluid, and let the flow continue at will.

If, after a while one simply drifts into a reverie about the everyday, try focusing on the yellow light again, but then immediately release control again. If the mind goes back to the subject matter that was previously occupying it, allow that. Judging the significance of thoughts or their implications is impossible. If the aim of the practice is to allow change then, by definition, one cannot control it. Knowing which change is appropriate and which is not is impossible, until a different perspective is firmly established. And that perspective might again change. One cannot label some thoughts significant and others insignificant. While engaged in the process, one cannot possibly analyze what comes to mind. The only course is to let it be.

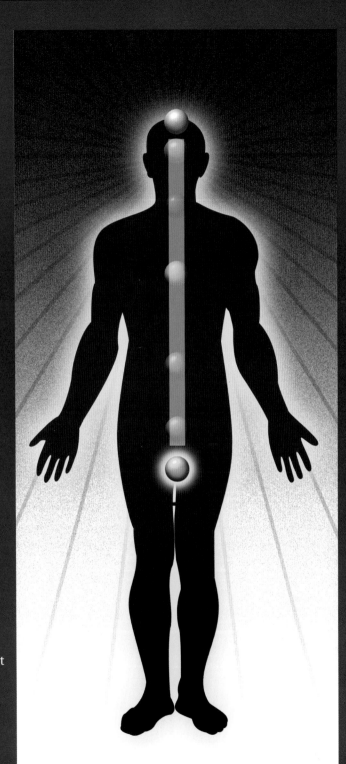

2. EXPERIENCING THE MEDITATION

Continue meditating in this way until reaching the end of a train of thought or the end of the desire or need for the exercise. This could occur within five minutes or take much longer. However, the amount of time spent is not relevant. A sense of having spent exactly the right length of time is all that is required. And the right time to spend on this meditation varies from person to person, and from session to session.

WHEN FEELING A SENSE OF COMPLETION, return the focus and the yellow chakra to the center of the forehead. Hold it there for an instant, and then begin the return journey down the body, back to the perineum.

REPLACE THE LIGHT in the chakra it came from. Now, switching off the light is crucial.

TURN OFF THE LIGHT. This is a very important step. If using the device of seeing a switch was effective, then use it again. For some people, simply "seeing" the light as going off is sufficient.

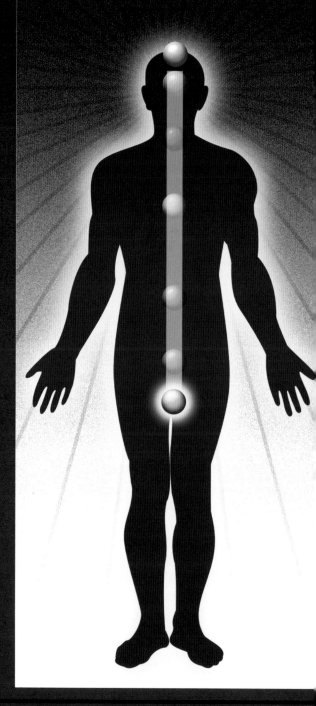

ENDING THE MEDITATION

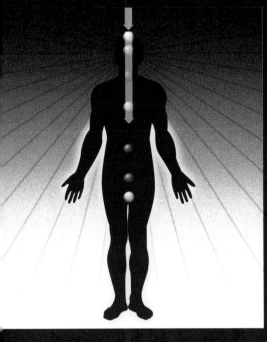

CLOSE THE CHAKRAS, once the light is extinguished. Making certain they are closed ensures that access to one's energy and energy centers is not unwittingly exposed. To make certain the chakras are closed, follow this simple procedure.

VISUALIZE A WHITE light in the shape of an arrow above the head.

FOLLOW THE ARROW to move quickly down through the body, along the line of the main chakras, from the crown down to the floor. Repeat this at least twice more, checking that there is no sign of light or activity.

FINALLY, GIVE THANKS. Open your eyes and prepare to record the practice, which is the next stage.

MOVING UP

The chakra meditation progresses from the first chakra to the second when the issues at the first chakra have been sufficiently explored. From the second chakra, it progresses to the third, and so on. In this way the issues and the energy at each chakra are explored. However, the time to move up is when there is a real need—not simply a desire—to do so.

As one develops the ability to work with the chakra meditation, the focus eventually progresses from the first chakra to the second. When the issues at the first chakra have been exhausted, each individual recognizes the right time to progress from the first chakra to the second. Once the cleansing of the second chakra is complete, the time comes to progress to the third chakra, and so on. This process allows the issues and the energy at each chakra to be explored. However, the time to move is when one recognizes a need–not simply a desire— to do so.

Desire can be dangerous. It can be a motivating force to press ahead in an unworthy attempt to achieve results—a concept that is contradictory. It is impossible to assess results. And any "results" are endangered by moving from one chakra to the next without having concentrated long enough on the prior one. If the journey is seen as a race to reach the heart, or the chakras above it, the results are inevitably disappointing. It is possible to progress through the chakras led only by desire, without any real change occurring.

The time to move from the base to the second chakra usually is clear. Sometimes, a sign from within the meditation itself prompts a move. Other times, there is the simple sense that it is time to make a move. The movement from the first to the second chakra, and in each successive case, is straightforward.

The process to move from the first to the second chakra is as follows.

NTER THE MEDITATION REALM as usual.

O TO THE BASE CHAKRA AND SWITCH IT ON
o see a yellow light), but do not pull the
ase chakra upwards.

OVE ON TO THE SECOND CHAKRA AND
WITCH THAT ON (to see a medium blue light).
may take a while to establish a color, but do
ot be concerned: That is not important.

AISE THE BLUE LIGHT TO THE MIDDLE OF THE
OREHEAD, to exactly the same position where
e base was raised, and continue to follow
e same procedure.

THE LIGHT to the center of the forehead.
FOCUS ON THE BLUE LIGHT, and allow it to
travel down the body, back to its correct place.

SWITCH IT OFF when it reaches its original place.

MOVE DOWN TO THE LIGHT OF THE CHAKRA
BELOW, in this case the base chakra, and
switch that off too.

VISUALISE A WHITE LIGHT IN THE SHAPE OF
AN ARROW, above the crown of the head.

BRING THE WHITE ARROW DOWN through
the crown, into the body, down to the base

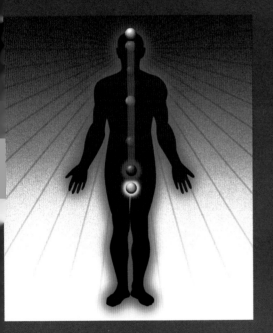

OCUS ON THE BLUE LIGHT FROM THE MIDDLE
OF THE FOREHEAD, then let it go. Allow the
nind to wander at will, without censuring
houghts or feelings.

VHEN THE PROCESS FEELS COMPLETE, RETURN

process aims to ensure all the chakras are
closed. It is best to repeat it at least three
times, taking care to make sure no signs of
light or its activity are still in the body.

GIVE THANKS.
Make a record of the practice, exactly as before.

ADVANCING

When the appropriate time comes to move from the second chakra to the third (or later, further up), the process is exactly the same as from the first to the second. The time spent working with each chakra may vary from as long as a few days to many months. Yet absolutely no benefit comes from rushing.

When entering the meditation realm, a lower chakra that appeared to be exhausted already sometimes may want to "come forward." In that case, allow that lower chakra to rise to the forehead, and concentrate on it for as long as necessary before proceeding to the next chakra.

The strength of the whole depends on the strength of each chakra, from the base upwards. Unless the structure is solid, from the base upwards, the effects are dramatically reduced.

When advancing from one chakra to the next, follow the same process, as repeated here.

TO BEGIN, enter the meditation realm as usual.

TO MOVE TO THE NEXT CHAKRA, switch on

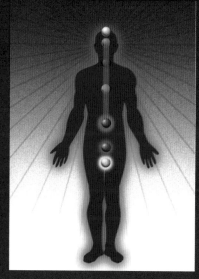

WHEN MOVING TO THE THIRD CHAKRA, switch on the base chakra and then the sexual chakra. Move up to the third chakra, which generates a red light. Guide it to the forehead.

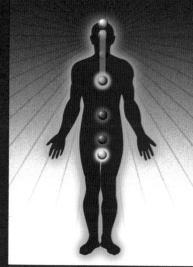

WHEN MOVING TO THE HEART CHAKRA, switch on the base chakra, sexual chakra, and third chakra. Move up to the heart chakra, which generates a green light. Guide it to the forehead.

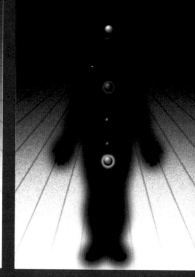

WHEN MOVING TO THE THROAT CHAKRA, switch on the base chakra, sexual chakra, third chakra, and heart chakra. Move up to the throat chakra, which generates a dark blue light. Guide it to the forehead.

e base chakra and continue switching on the
akras above it until reaching the new chakra.

OVE UP TO THE NEW CHAKRA and switch
at on to see its light. (It may take a while.)

AISE THE LIGHT to the middle of the forehead,
d focus on it there. Then let it go, allowing
e mind to wander at will, without censure.

HEN COMPLETE, RETURN THE LIGHT to the center
the forehead. Focus on it, allowing it to travel
own the body, back to its correct place.

SWITCH IT OFF when it reaches its original place.

MOVE DOWN TO THE CHAKRA below and switch
that off, then do the same for the chakras below.

ALWAYS FINISH BY SEEING AN ARROW OF WHITE
LIGHT above the head and pulling it down several
times through all the chakras to make certain
they are all closed.

OFFER A PRAYER of thanks.

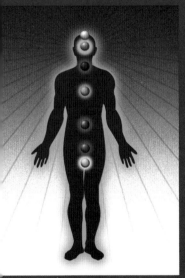

HEN MOVING TO THE SIXTH
HAKRA, switch on the base
hakra, sexual chakra, third
hakra, heart chakra, and throat
hakra. Move up to the sixth
hakra, which generates an
range light. Allow it to radiate
own light in the forehead.

WHEN MOVING TO THE CROWN
CHAKRA, switch on the base
chakra, sexual chakra, third
chakra, heart chakra, throat
chakra, and sixth chakra. Move
up to the crown chakra, which
generates a white light. This
light spreads above the head

ALWAYS FINISH BY SEEING AN
ARROW OF WHITE LIGHT above
the crown chakra and pulling it
down several times through each
chakra to make certain that they
are all closed. Remember to do
this at the end of every chakra
meditation session, regardless

RECORDING EACH MEDITATION

Diaries are partial. They reflect both the writer's perspective and desires. For example, to record thoughts and feelings that cannot be expressed in the outside world, or to keep notes of meetings, or even to impress future generations of potential readers. In short, diaries are written to fulfill many different functions.

A meditation diary is an important part of this meditation process. However, keeping this diary has a rather unusual, yet specific, aim—to avoid being selective when writing. The diary is intended to be a record of each individual meditation session. It need not be detailed, but should sketch roughly the course of the meditation.

Given that the aim of the entire process is to widen perception and to inspire change, intention and interpretation are dangerous games. Any interpretation comes from a particular perspective. It may be exactly that position that needs to change, or simply will change. As a result, it is difficult to judge what to include as significant, and what to exclude as insignificant. In general it is better to include what seems trivial than to exclude it. The links or logic between a string of visions that include, for example, lunch, a laundry list, a childhood event, and a seascape may not be evident at all, but omitting one of those images could significantly alter the whole.

This exercise of recording the meditation practice is not, however, to enable the material to be analyzed. On the contrary, it is important not to analyze it. Instead, the reason for recording the exercise is to formally acknowledg or "fix," the events that occur. In other words, to make sure that they are recognized by the mind before releasing them. Going back over diary

tes can be counterproductive. It is not possible
analyze your meditation journey while you are
aveling. Like any journey, it is important to
joy and experience it to the fullest while
aveling. It is not until later that the effects
the journey reveal themselves in full.
If I had tried to analyze my own seated
editation journey at the start, I would have
led it. I could not have understood what was
ppening. All the ways that I tried to interpret
—through the church, by investigating
ferences to mythology, through Buddhist
quiry—drew blanks, and fury from the
ages that populated my journey.
e message was clear: no
terpretation. I also sensed
e importance of not
tempting, at this stage,
find others to explain

what was happening, or to allow them to impose
their interpretations. I needed to experience the
journey. Only later, in some cases years later, did
I begin to understand what had happened. Often
my understanding has increased from one year
to the next, as my perspective has widened, and
I have become able to see more, for
which I am immensely grateful.

REMEMBER WHAT'S IMPORTANT

The aim of the chakra meditation is to help one to connect with the deepest self and the
rest of the universe. It works by releasing obstacles and blocks that are lodged in, and
limiting, the body's energy.

1. **PLACE, TIME, FREQUENCY,** and
   preparedness—all of these help to
   establish the most positive circumstances.

2. **SAYING A PRAYER** is essential to connect
   with the Divine and the rest of creation.

3. **TRUST THAT MEDITATION** works. The
   experience is supported by the belief that
   it works.

4. **PRACTICING MEDITATION** is not about
   success or failure. One cannot judge what
   success or failure is, especially while
   engaged in the process.

5. **ONE MUST CONCENTRATE** only on personal
   experience. That is all that matters. Weaving
   fantasies, imagining visions, using the models of
   others' experiences—all that serves no purpose.

6. **STOP AS SOON** as the feeling comes that
   it is time to stop.

7. **RECORD THE PRACTICE** unselectively.

9. **MAKE THE PRACTICE** a habit for as long as
   it feels desirable or necessary.

10. **ENJOY IT.** Meditation is a great adventure
    into the most fascinating of unknown
    territories.

He who doubts from what he sees

Will ne'er believe, do what you please.

If Sun and Moon should doubt,

They'd immediately go out.

—William Blak

"Thel's Motto," *The Book of Th*

DEVELOPING TRUST

The first problem for those who are unsure in attempting the meditation is the obvious—the sense that nothing is happening. That the chakra will not come alight. That it is impossible to start the process. The answer is equally simple, enormously difficult to achieve, and hugely effective. Trust. The trust that the process will occur, and produce results, is the key to enabling it to do exactly that. As ever, doubt is eminently effective as a self-fulfilling prophecy. Sometimes the chakra does not burst into a blaze of light. But there is a sense of a color, or a sense of light, that is more than enough to start the process. And practice strengthens the process. It is one of the chief reasons why regularity and frequency are so important, combined with the intention to meditate and

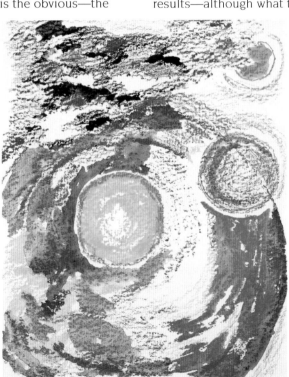

SUN, MOON, AND BEYOND
A picture of the planets

the expectation that the meditation will produce results—although what those results will be cannot be known in advance. Trust is the surest way to guarantee the outcome.

Failure is another red herring. There is no failure. Even if the chakra does not display even a faint tinge of light or color, the attempt produces results. It strengthens the practice. It reinforces the intention to meditate effectively, and reinforces the desire to repeat the effort—as long as it is not considered or labelled as a failure. It is an attempt that, in itself, can be considered a success. Every day produces another opportunity for an attempt. Continuing is all important. Gradually, perhaps imperceptibly, continuing in this way eventually produces results. Trust is the key to a successful outcome.

LIGHT & DARK

The stars on a dark night are beautiful. A deep indigo sky tells the story of the hidden depths of the universe. Yet, like a child, sometimes one fears the qualities that are bundled together under the label of The Dark. Meeting the dark, in whatever form it manifests, presents above all the need to remember that light and dark are two sides of the same coin. The Chinese symbol of the yin and yang illustrates precisely this intertwined nature.

It is the experience of the dark that enables the light to shine. At the same time, everyone is composed of both light and dark qualities. All life is a complex mixture of shades from light

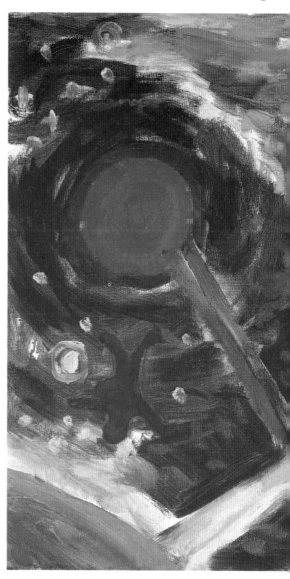

dark, just as it is composed of cycles that
ove from birth to death and back again—in
spheres of existence.

From time to time, the chakra meditation brings
at dark to the surface. On these occasions, it is
ten composed of buried fears, pain, anger, envy—
d wounds deeply lodged in the body's energy.
uring meditation these issues, or the marks
at they have left behind in one's energy, may
e encountered and re-lived. It can produce

experiences best described as meeting "the dark."
This may manifest as visions of frightening
situations in some ways reminiscent of the
original experiences. Or perhaps as encounters
with a figure or figures who arouse fear, again
related to past dark situations.

When issues are buried particularly deeply,
a more complex process sometimes takes place.
This is the process known in psychotherapy as
"projection." In such cases, unwelcome qualities
that cannot be acknowledged in the
self are projected onto another who
is seen as "dark," or even as a "devil"
figure. When this happens in
meditation (or in dreams), the dark
figure or figures are usually aspects
of oneself. For example, if one has
repeated experiences in life of
feeling fierce aggression towards
others that is not acknowledged or
understood, the meditation may
reveal an encounter with another who
is behaving in a fierce, threatening,
and aggressive way. That does not
represent a situation where a threat
is coming from the outside. Rather,
it may be a way of showing how the
behavior is being elicited from within.

On other occasions the experience
of meeting the dark may reflect the
experience of encountering what can
be called "dark forces" in the universe.
Individuals meet or help create these
forces constantly. They can vary from
confronting the active ill intent of
another, to the confusion and bad
temper caused by a traffic jam.
Dealing with the dark requires a
little skill.

HE FELL
A picture of a dark event

MEETING THE LIGHT & THE DARK

Encountering the dark is part of a natural cycle, the cycle of the earth. However, it can cause fear or confusion, which inhibits this flow from light to dark. The fear is caused by holding onto wounds in one's energy—the old pains that one carries. These energetic markers dictate behavior and keep one, to a degree, in the power of the dark.

The chakra meditation encourages inner change, which means allowing the dark trapped in the body's energy to come to the surface. When it does, there are good ways of dealing with it. Facing the dark as it surfaces, it is best to stand, metaphorically speaking, as peacefully as possible before it. The dark is rarely overcome by combat. Acknowledgement and understanding are the keys to embracing it. In that way fear, anxieties, past hurts, and their energetic markers, all of which are the constituents of the dark—and create vulnerablity—can be relinquished, allowing

ght to be reestablished. Where the dark that lodged in one's own energy is projected onto someone else, recognizing that fact, rather than ghting it by seeing the other as the enemy, is he only method to disperse it.

Similarly, if the dark is a genuine manifestation f an outside force, there is rarely—though I cannot ay never—a case for fighting it. Remaining as still nd peaceful as possible is usually the most effective ay of withstanding such encounters. Also much can e learned from considering the nature of the dark. hat makes a situation frightening? Or destructive? lmost always part of the answer lies in oneself. he root of the dark may even be in projection. ncovering and digesting that information is an ssential part of developing understanding.

Just as meeting the dark can cause anxiety, heeting the light can give rise to bliss. That bliss ; magical. It can be no more and no less than the most blinding sense of inner love that contact ith the spiritual reality sometimes offers. This uality, like radiant light, is often hugely desired, highly prized, and much sought after. So much so that it may be created in imagination, as part of blocking out an inevitably more checkered reality. Needless to say, this is a futile exercise. Intense experiences of light are part of the huge, multi-layered cycle of life. Often the real experience of light can only be as intense as the willingness (not the necessity) to experience dark. At the same time, like summer, light cannot be held onto.

Concentrating only on light is potentially as unbalancing as concentrating only on dark. Blissful light experiences should be treasured and valued. But craving blissful experiences can make less radiant experiences seem more painful, and invariably cause distress. Light and dark both have their place. Each has something to offer. In time the light becomes less blinding, the dark less threatening, the whole more peaceful, happy, and ultimately transcendent.

Practicing meditation is not about seeking exotic experiences, but about finding balance, harmony, and true joy in life.

MEDITATION & CREATIVITY

Creativity is a part of the human birthright. Increasingly, creativity is seen as essential in all spheres of life, from business to medicine, and as a key ingredient of a joyful, productive life. However, many people view creativity as a distant attainment or an elite possession.

To many, creativity is a special talent that manifests itself only in chosen individuals under favored circumstances. In truth, creativity requires nothing but a certain type of freedom. The constraints that block true creativity are the exact constraints that the chakra meditation aims to remove. They are the limiting energetic patterns, the ways in which old wounds, negative experiences, fears, and frustrations are held. Freeing oneself from those old hurts, or at least releasing oneself from their paralyzing effects, allows a new route to creativity to emerge. The poet William Wordsworth understood very well the inhibiting effects of certain experiences. In "Resolution and Independence"(1807) he writes:

> I *shook the habit off*
> *Entirely and forever, and again*
> *In Nature's presence stood, as I now stand,*
> *A sensitive being, a creative soul.*

At the same time that the chakra meditation releases old energetic patterns, it also helps deepen or enliven creativity by reaching towards levels of consciousness that are not often accessed. It does so because the aim of meditation is not to produce exotic experiences, but ultimately to go beyond experiences to reach the unconscious or the deeper dimension. Then it opens a way to allow this level to unravel, and even deeper depth to emerge. Inevitably, the entire process acts as a spur to creativity.

MESSAGE FROM MY DEEPER SELF

My own meditation journey has gone hand in hand with bursts of activity in my creative life. At various times, paintings, which often have names, or even "stories," attached to them have come to me. In one case in 1992, I painted a rather simplistic self-portrait that was actually predictive, though I was not able to read it at the time.

The picture is harsh, with hard lines and simple shapes. On the stylized shape that represents the face, on the lower half of the right-hand side, I painted a large circular white shape that looks somewhat like a snowball. I had no idea what it represented, and didn't even consider the question. Then I found the whole image uncomfortable to look at (too harsh, I thought) and hid the picture in an obscure corner. It was not pleasing for me to look at, but it *was* something else.

In fact, the picture was an image from my deeper consciousness, which was trying to show me something. It was trying, as clearly as it could,

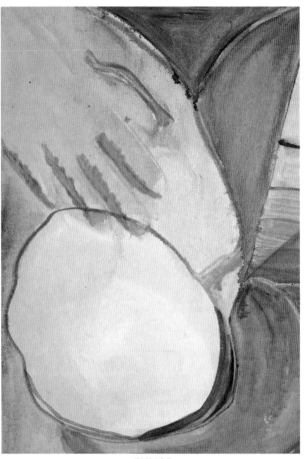

TUMOR

to show me the presence of the tumor that was threatening my life. The large "snowball" on the lower right-hand side was the tumor that was identified and removed two years later. It was situated exactly as the picture shows, on the lower right-hand side. While not snowball size, the tumor was huge—the size of a peach. Yet I did not see what I had painted at the time.

Meditation can have an equally profound effect on other types of creative arts, such as writing and music, and on all other spheres of life, from business to private life. Teaching a weekend course that included a great deal of meditation and work on its role in creativity, I was compelled to write a novel afterwards! Often I have watched clients' solutions to work and personal problems become increasingly creative and well-grounded as their meditation settles into a consistent practice. It seems they are freed from old, inhibiting patterns of thought and feeling.

CONTEMPLATION

Most people benefit from

meditation at some stage,

but the chakra meditation

does not necessarily

need to be an ongoing or

continuous process. There

may be times when the

chakra meditation is not

desirable or appropriate,

for any one of a number

of reasons.

Contemplation allows one's mind to wander, to float like a bird. It can be encouraged by the natural world, but also practiced in very ordinary, external situations.

In my own case, if meditation had been suggested at any earlier stage in my life, I would have refused point-blank to try it. I would not have been able to see its relevance, and I would not have felt drawn to try it. However, a particular type of daydreaming had always been part of my life. Quiet times, whether occupied by repetitive domestic chores, spent in nature, or simply enjoyed in solitude, were and are essential to my sense of well-being. In hindsight, I can say that daydreaming, or its other name "contemplation," has always been part of my routine.

Contemplation can offer an alternative path toward the unstructured depths. In its own way, contemplation is just as important as meditation. According to the poet Milton in Il Penseroso:

> And Wisdom's self
> Oft seeks to sweet retired solitude
> Where with her best nurse Contemplation
> She plumes her feathers, and lets grow her wings.

Contemplation does not necessarily mean "doing nothing." Any repetitive action, from vacuuming to painting a wall, can allow or encourage contemplation. The essential ingredient is a certain mental freedom where minimal attention is required to complete the task in hand, leaving the mind utterly free. For some, listening to music has the same effect as contemplation (or even meditation). Listening to music can free the mind in the same way as contemplation and can stimulate the ability to write or to make music. For others, silence is essential.

TEACHERS & TRANSMISSION

The role of leader or teacher is much debated in all spheres of life, from school rooms to business practices to politics. The teacher can even play a part in contemplation, and much more so in meditation. This is true for solo activities or group practice. Teachers and leaders wield great influence.

Raphael's painting shows the school of Athens, which followe the pursuit of higher learning with religious devotion.

Spiritual life is no exception. The teachings of a leader, the way that a leader exercises authority, an the example he or she sets for acceptable behavior are all particularly important.

We are living in exciting and challenging times. We face great uncertainty as well as opportunities in our world. In some areas we are questioning the role and content of leadership. Relationships with teachers and leaders to whom we look for inspiration and guidance are also under scrutiny. In the spiritual sphere this has implications with potentially enormous positive consequences.

We are moving out of the age of the old-style spiritual prophet whose role was to bring the word of a god to the people. Instead, we are

The panel, from a fresco by Fra Angelico, depicts Christ as he delivers the Sermon on the Mount.

oving into a stage where, though leadership
mains important for guidance and inspiration, we
ant to take responsibility in a new, profound way.
Many people are experiencing an urge to find
pirituality. For many, studying the words of a guru
nd following them simply because they are given
no longer enough. It is important to be guided
y one's own inner sense: to check whether what
he hears in the outer world resonates with one's
wn deepest inner feelings. This requires assuming
creased personal responsibility. For many, it is
o longer enough to give up responsibility and act
olely according to the dictates of a guru or leader.
his approach has implications for many aspects of
e, like business and politics as well as spirituality.
At the same time, teachers and leaders continue
o be very important. However, understanding
nergy makes it clear that everyone is linked.
teractions from personal relations to world
conomics show this fact: All people influence one
nother. This means that in choosing and following
aders and teachers we need to have both better
nderstanding and greater responsibility.
We are influenced not only by the words our
aders say, but by their actions and intentions.
ltimately, the energy of a leader or teacher—
e whole of that person—has great influence.
technical terms, the mechanics of energetic
ansmission are at work. The old saying
ead by example" is true in the widest
ossible sense. The example of
adership pervades not only
ne's thoughts, but one's very
nergy, influencing behavior
many different ways.
he reality of transmission
emands special authenticity
nd integrity from teachers and
aders. It also gives each person

the particular responsibility to follow his or her
own intuition in assessing those in positions of
authority or power.

Working to develop spirituality and awareness,
a teacher with whom one shares a true energetic
link can be a great help in furthering an individual's
development. Not only are the teacher's ideas
beneficial, but his or her energy itself has a powerful
effect. The more powerful the teacher, the greater
the energetic effect, or transmission of energy. If
that energy is benevolent and expansive, the gain
from sharing it will be considerable.

Because a teacher can have such a powerful effect,
discrimination in choosing a teacher is essential.
A link with a teacher should be a means to greater
independence, not a reason to give up one's
independence. This idea has an important part
to play in the organization of the family, society,
business, politics, and personal relations.

he 14th Dalai Lama, Tenzin Gyatso,
ceived the Nobel Peace Prize in 1989.

GUIDED
JOURNEYS

3

Once individual practice is established,
meditation as part of a group can be
fun. Sharing experiences and energy
with others can increase the benefits
and pleasures. The right group provides
a joyful, supportive atmosphere.
Remember, though, never to compare
experiences competitively. Each has a
different journey. Swapping experiences
can be useful. Judging them is always
destructive—and impossible. Of course,
leadership influences the outcome too.

Many activities go under the label

of group meditations. When I work

with groups of people who are already

familiar with the chakra meditation,

I sometimes lead what I call

"inspirational meditation journeys."

I set a scene for the group with my

words, then encourage them to follow

in their own private meditations.

GROUP WORK

t the same time, the reality of energy and
ansmission means that I am sharing my energy
th the group—just as
ey all share theirs. To
ant, the effect feels as
ough I am inviting
em to travel with me.
If the group members
spond to my energy and
e energy we create as a
hole, they are able to go
eper into themselves.
ur combined energy
lows them to travel
rther and more
werfully than they could
they were meditating on
eir own. Also, the
rection in which they
avel is influenced by my
ergy. They might go in
different direction if they
ere sitting with another
ader. Afterwards, each
ember of the group
scusses his or her individual meditation. If they
k, I offer my intuitive interpretations of their
avels. Some of these accounts follow.

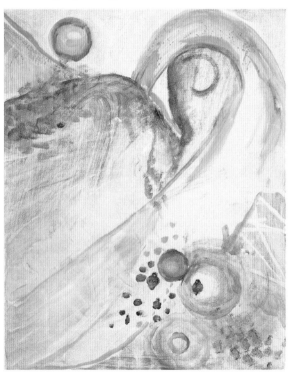

UNIVERSAL PATHWAY
This represents the interconnectedness of humans.

When leading these groups, the language I
use is sometimes a little unusual. For this
reason, I have edited
the descriptions that
follow to make them
easier to read. Aside
from those minor
revisions, the journeys
described here are
based on actual
meditation sessions.
They are taken from
groups I have led and
accounts of individual
clients' experiences.
I have changed their
names and omitted or
altered any personal
details that could
make the individual
identifiable.
Reading them, the
experiences of members
of this group may sound
familiar. Often, the
images revealed in internal journeys are
shared by many, suggesting that no one
truly travels alone.

GROUP MEDITATION

It is a damp, chilly London evening. When the members of the group begin to arrive, the early evening winter sky is already pitch black. On arriving, each leaves his or her shoes in the hall, enters the room silently, and finds a seat in the large circle. Altogether, fourteen of us gather tonight. There are smiles and nods, but few words. To one side, three candles are burning. I lit three because in so many systems of thought, from

Christianity to the tarot, the number three has a special significance—from the Holy Trinity to the fruitful union, to the essential unity of body, mind and spirit.

In a corner of the room a large vase is filled with a combination of fresh flowers and greenery. Aesthetically they are a source of great pleasure. At the same time, the vibration, or energy, of the leaves and flowers is helpful. The clear, clean water in the large vase also is useful for absorbing negativity. Earlier in the day, the door and all the windows of the room were opened and the space thoroughly "aired." I do not use incense or aromatherapy oil on these occasions. The combined effect of the group's presence is strong enough.

Once everyone has arrived, the silence deepens. The time to start has come. I greet the group. To enable everyone to rise to the highest spiritual level of which they are capable at present, I must even out the energy in the group. In practical terms, that means that as energy circulates around the group, its smooth flow can be interrupted if two or more people with particularly low, or especially high, energy sit beside each other. Their energy can form a dip or a hill. Many factors may be involved. For example, male energy and female energy differ. Each individual carries a particular assortment of qualities, or energies, so all of these factors need to be balanced for this evening's experience. (There are occasions when it is important for those who choose to sit together to do so, but this is not one of them.) I see or feel the energies involved and ask everyone to swap places until I am satisfied that the group is arranged properly. Then we begin.

We start the evening with a prayer. Personally, I like to use the word God, but many other words would do equally well, such as "The Creative," or "The Light," or "The Source." Remember that my words may sound unusual because my state is heightened.

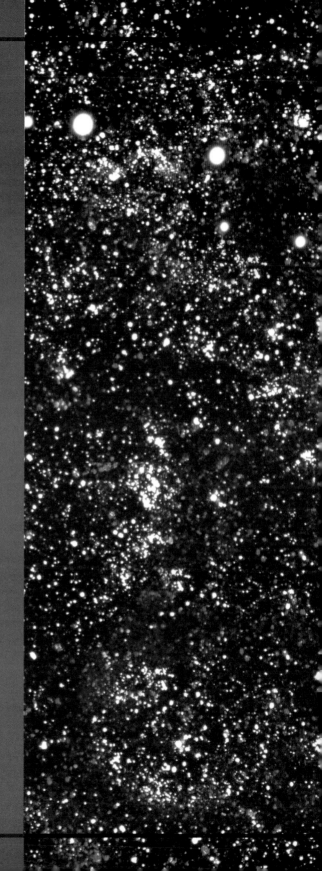

GROUP MEDITATION PREPARATION

"First, I'm going to make some general points. On these particular evenings, remember whenever possible: Bathe, change your clothes, avoid strong smells, and avoid alcohol or other drugs. Cleanse yourself in the ways that you know best.

"Next, remember that whatever anyone says this evening is said in the moment. I do not hold anyone to anything they say, nor should you. The purpose of the evening is revelation and change. What is so at the start of the evening may not be so by the end of the evening. Anything anyone says is therefore no more and no less than a reflection of a particular moment.

At all times this evening, avoid personality. Avoid all issues of who and whom. Allow yourself to be present in your highest form. Be present simply as Love. Offer love to those around you without judgement. Do not consider whom it is that you speak to or for or beside. Know only your love for those around you. See yourself as a mirror. Those attitudes that arise in you towards others, are your own. Do not see them as a manifestation of the other. All reactions are you: The pain, the anger, the fear you feel from them, those are all yours too."

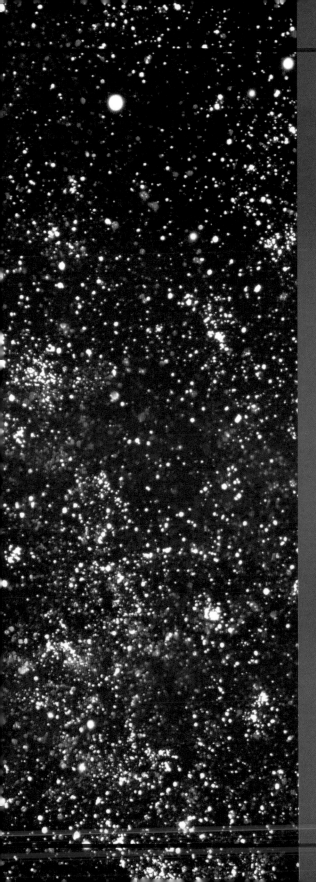

❖

Your intelligence is always with you,
Overseeing your body, even though
You may not be aware of its work.

You and your intelligence
Are like beauty and the precision
Of an astrolabe.

Together you calculate how near
Existence is to the sun!

Your intelligence is marvelously intimate.
It's not in front of you or behind,
Or to the left or the right.

Now try my friend, to describe how near
Is the creator of your intellect!

Intellectual searching will not find
The way to that king!

There are guides who can show you the way.
Use them. But they will not satisfy your longing.
Keep wanting that connection
With all your pulsing energy.

Observe the wonders as they occur around you.
Don't claim them. Feel the artistry
Moving through, and be silent.

—

JELALUDDIN RUMI (B. 1207)
Words taken from *Body Intelligence*

❖

MEDITATION JOURNEY

"Concentrate your minds and see above you a White Light. It is white for God, for love, for spirit, for infinity, forever. And it moves in a counterclockwise direction, the rays radiating to the earth. They pierce your body and your heart, they speak in words and syllables and sounds that your deepest, deepest feelings respond to. Your mind has no knowledge. Let your heart listen, let your body respond as it would. Know that the White Light that pierces you is the White Light that pierces all of humanity, all of the earth, all flowers, all fauna, all flora, all creatures, and all dimensions. You are connected.

It moves around and around. Now, in front of the White Light, a Blue Light appears. It is blue for healing. The Blue Light glows softly as it moves in a clockwise direction. The blue beams bathe you. They offer forgiveness to every cell of your body. They teach patience and love and unfolding. All the parts that ache are bathed. All the parts of you too deep to speak their pain are touched.

Give yourself to the Blue Light, offer to accept the shape that you should be, let that shape be yours. Offer that you will embrace the freedom that is yours. Say and do as you dare not. Allow the limits to be beyond your concepts. Embrace the non-conceptual infinit that faces you in love and light and healing, in alignment, in a sense of which you have no understanding. Give to God, that God may give to you.

Now in the Blue Light, remember those closest, dearest, furthest, and of least importance. And offer them these pleasures too. Feel the pain of others singing in your

ars, as it links with your own, as you link
ith them. Pride and arrogance shrivel and
ou know the totality of humanity; hold it in
our hands.

Now, you prepare to enter your innermost
omain. You are completely safe and secure
nd at any point, should you so wish, you may
urn away from the depths that beckon. Ask
o go to the place or places where your
resence is most needed.

Now follow the words, and move down into
our soul domain.

Take the first step. And the mists swirl
round you, and your links with the everyday

grow fainter now. Step back again, a second
time. It is your own interior calling you. And
a third step and a fourth step.

Check that your physical body sits still, that
it feels at rest, that your back, the conduit
of your energy, is at peace.

And hurry now, the fifth step deeper yet.
And the sixth, and the seventh, and your
blood calls you now: arms outstretched to
meet you, what you cannot see; the eighth
and the ninth.

Now a stairway opens beyond. Down the
stairs, you are deep, deep in another realm.
And you open the door and find yourself in
the place you find yourself.

Now follow where you are led, follow where
your fancy and your need take you. See what
there is to see, let what will be, be.

Use no influence in this place, simply allow
and accept the interior.

Go well."

MEDITATION JOURNEY

For several minutes the group travels, each in his or her own world, in meditation. Now it is time to bring them back.

"The mist swirls thickly around you. It is time to leave the place or places you have visited. So make your way back, slowly, now carrying the lessons you have learnt, or simply the things you have seen, back with you. Do not judge. Do not condemn or hurry to embrace. Let the knowledge be with you and be, in time, what it will.

"And as you make your way back to the place where you entered, you will know that your access to this domain is in your control.

"Now open the door, and go up the stairs.

"When you're ready, take the first step.

"And the second step, and the air is clear and cool. It is night time, stars are in the sky.

"And the third and the fourth step: You can feel the chill and the dampness around you. And the sixth and the seventh, and you pass the glare of electric lights. And the eighth and the ninth bring you to your place, and your everyday consciousness assumes control. Now when you are ready, open your eyes."

I pause for a few minutes while everyone emerges, opens their eyes, and rests for a few moments.

"OK. Good to see you all. We'll go around the group now and anyone who has anything to say, please do so. If you'd like me to comment, I will.

"Jay, you're first."

PERSONAL JOURNEYS

SITTING ON A STAR

"I felt very moved as I went down through the steps. Then, when the door opened, it was into—just emptiness: midnight blue emptiness and stars. The perspective was infinite and yet the stars were also like stepping stones. I felt I was meant to do very little but that my breathing was important. And that there was a pulse in the stars, like the pulse of breath. I felt I could sit on a star, and it was very comfortable: this infinity, this emptiness.

"Then I saw a group of Light figures who came and sat around on the stars too, and part of me wondered whether it was appropriate to continue sitting. But it was. Eventually one figure—it wasn't really a figure, just an overwhelming sense of goldness—supported me, and we stood opposite one another. All the Light figures came closer and there was an embrace which was very freeing. I had to just focus on their eyes and receive the Light from the eyes—forever, it felt like.

"It was quite difficult at first, to maintain that level of focus and that intensity. At one point we became one and then like a swirl, like a spiral, and I could feel the temptation to fly right through the center of the spiral. But I also felt, 'Not right now, but maybe at some point it would be appropriate.' Why was that?"

'The eyes are the windows to the soul, which connects with the universe and with all others at a soul level, as all souls merge into the spiral. When you are on earth, an "earth dweller," so to speak, and you really touch the spiritual domain, there is sometimes the temptation to give up all else for it. There is the desire to be 'just spiritual' in some way, without the messy issues of being human. It is essential not to give way to that longing. While you have a human body, the concerns of the flesh must be yours! So though you're shown the other dimension, you are not asked to join it yet. Only, of course, to do what is so important: to honor the spiritual dimension in every way in your life on earth."

'The meditation went on. I had more of a sense of a softer, feminine energy with lots of green, which was enjoyable and cleansing and fresh. I felt like I had a good wash in it. Then it was over. What was the green?"

'It is as if the meditation was bringing you right back into the green growth of the earth, and showing you how much it has to offer. So the spiritual domain is wonderful, but the earth has many delights too.

"Thank you, Jay. Sara's next."

A ROLE TO PLAY

"I went to two places at once: I went to Africa, and to another place that I've been to before which believe it or not is close to where I live, except I felt the sand was very pink and the people very tall. But in the vision of Africa, I was going back to my village where I lived and holding an African child who was starving. All I had to do was sit and be with the child. Then my stomach opened, and I was able to feed the people in the village from it somehow. Everything was very red and brown and ocher—really lovely colors. It made me feel rooted and well."

"Yes, lovely Sara. Do you want me to say anything?"

"Yes, please."

"Well, I feel in your meditation, Africa is a metaphor that contains two dimensions. First there is Africa, the real place, and then Africa, the energetic vibration, which you also see close to where you live. You're in two places at once because you're often in two places at once. Since both places hold the same vibration for you, you are connected to both of them. Most of us are linked in some way to many different places. Your meditation is telling you that these two places have something in common for you.

"Interestingly, you recognize that the Africa you connect with is starving and that you have the ability to feed it, from yourself. At the same time, you see that

n connecting with Africa, you connect with strong earth energy, which is particularly represented in those colors. And they are also the colors of nourishment, of food, and of the solar plexus, the third chakra. So you're saying, 'I recognize my job. I recognize that my job is to feed others on earth and to feed that particular vibration. Which is also how I will be nourished.'

"It doesn't necessarily apply just to the physical location, Africa. There are other places with similar vibrations, or elements of similar vibrations. There are also others who resonate to those vibrations. Because you are able to sense that particular energetic vibration so clearly, you are especially able to connect with the individuals all over the earth who pick up that vibration. It's the entire vibration, as well as those who resonate to it, which you are especially connected with. This is your particular responsibility and privilege.

"Going back to Africa—the place—will be wonderful because it will re-energize you. Every time you go back to Africa you will connect with that particular earthly vibration. It's as if you'll get a shot of, 'Remember, this is what you've got to do.' You'll be able to bring that back and continue to work with it—literally working from the gut.

"You also looked wonderful while you were meditating: very steady, solid energy. Thank you.

"Now, next, John. Don't worry if you didn't have nearly as coherent an experience as the other two—this is new for you. Jay and Sara have been at it for a long time."

THE EMOTIONAL LIGHT

"I found myself in several different places. The first was in an underground cavern with moss and water all over the walls. All the places I visited were very dark inside. In the cavern, there was a fox or a wolf. I don't know, I kept trying to find out if it had something to say to me and I couldn't quite understand if it did.

"Another place I visited was some kind of a forest. I wasn't on a path or anything. I was just...somewhere, staring up through amazingly tall trees, looking at the sky and the stars. The sky was like a sort of sunset but it was also dark, the way it is after dusk: There were still oranges and a whole rainbow of colors in the sky. It was like a rainforest.

"I also found myself in a very, very long dark tunnel that went down and down and down into the earth for many miles. It was like a road or an alley going down and down, and I was just traveling downwards on it. *Although it was so dark everywhere, I wasn't really scared in any of the places."*

"Thank you. Do you want me to say anything about your meditation?"

"Yes."

"You are working at the emotional level, which is where you ought to be working. Your heart has suffered and you need to work on repairing it. I think you'll find that there are issues connected with your father that are particularly occupying you at the moment. You might also find that you have physical chest symptoms, around here [indicates the chest area].

"Now the three images are all places that you are visiting on an emotional level. In the first, you move into the cavern. Of course, the cavern is the cavern inside you. There is a creature there—a creature who is often hunted, feared, and despised, but you are not afraid of that creature. However, you cannot set up a dialogue with that creature, or discover what it has to say. I suspect that creature is you. Also, it seems that you are keeping yourself separate from that creature—in other words, detached from yourself, or the wolf in you who could be wild and untamed, even dangerous, but also strong, clever, and a great survivor. Or from the fox in you, with all his qualities. If you could connect with the wild animal, you could have the power of those qualities at your disposal too.

"The second image says more about your detachment, and also speaks of lack of direction. You are in the forest. You're not following a path or on a track,

but you are surrounded by trees:
very tall trees. That suggests to me
that you feel there are many issues
all around you. You look up. It's as
if you feel your salvation will come
from above. 'Up' does indeed
provide glorious sights: rainbows
and a very emotive dusk. For most
people, dusk is a time when the
feelings are very open
to impressions of beauty and
sensitivity. You are capable of
wonderful feelings, and a strong
connection with the non-material
realms, which is a real blessing.

"However, what is important
for you at the moment is not to
go 'up' now, but rather to live life
on earth. You need to find your
way through the forest, to sort
out what the issues confronting
you are, and then to enjoy the
bounty of the earth, along with
your fine sensitivity—all of which
you can do.

"The third vision shows your
efforts to go into yourself and
resolve your personal issues. It
also shows that you are successful.
The tunnel that you have to go
down is accessible, and you are
able to travel down it unimpeded.
You actually have a way down
deeper into yourself. You've found
the way down. Your meditation
suggests that you have sufficient
security and presence of mind to
go down the tunnel. Well done.

"Next, please. Ruth."

REVIEWING YOUR SITUATION

"Well, I visited a kaleidoscope of places so I'll pick out the key ones I remember. I started off in a cav that was like the entrance to me. Then I was on a seashore, looking at the sea. On a couple of occasions, I was sitting looking out across the desert. It seemed that my eyes were very blue, when in reality my eyes are brown. I came back to the cave a couple of times, and there was a leopard pacing up and down. But it was chained up, so I wasn't frightened of it.

"Then I went to what seemed like some native ritual, where a spear was thrown into my heart, but it wasn't painful. At one point, I found myself in a place that was like a prison, where there were lots of women with cowls over their heads, rather like they wear in Middle Eastern countries. There were bars on the window, but there was a light shining through. I felt as though, 'There's always a light even in the darkest circumstances.'

"At another point I found myself walking down into water. It was very green and clear. Then I went under the water and through a door. That suggested Atlantis to me, and I looked over the landscape. At one stage, I was in a little enclosed space, like the space in a monastery, where centuries ago monks used to spend time doing penance. A little enclosed space. I had a kind of sideways view and it seemed there were lots of these tiny cocoons with people in them. And I thought, 'I can' fit into a space any smaller than this.' But later on I wa in a space where I was lying down, it was so narrow. It was even smaller than where I had been before.

"The final image was like a Biblical image of a whole host of people journeying across a desert and I was one of them. I can't remember anything else."

hank you, Ruth. Do you want
put from me?"

e nods.

's the final image that
nches it. You are reviewing
ur situation in a number of
fferent places. First, in the
ve that you recognize as
e depths of yourself. Also
 the seashore, which is the
omain of your personal
notions. And overall in
e journey of life.

"To begin with, at the
eashore you survey your
notions. But you don't
ander into the water—your
notions—until later on.
stead, you enter into some
ort of native ritual—like life,
erhaps? And you suffer from a
ound from a spear—perhaps
e are talking here of practical
roblems or a restriction.

"From there, you move to
prison. In some sense you
ee yourself as imprisoned,
erhaps trapped in your
entity. But how do you see
urself trapped in identity?
ot just trapped as a woman,
seems to be wider than that.
here is light in the women's
rison. You say there is always
ght, even in a prison. You are
ise. Then the sea takes over.

"Now you enter more fully
e world of your emotions.

You walk through a door
into what seems like a lost
civilization. This is the world
of your deeper emotions. Your
response is to see yourself as
a monk. As a monk—cloaked
in that identity—you feel truly
trapped, as if you are doing
penance. You see many others
who are similarly trapped. You
feel so trapped, it is as if your
identity—your personality, who
you are—is squashed into a
very small space. You feel you
can't squash yourself into a
space that is any smaller, but
later you do.

"Next, perhaps as a result of,
and trying to deal with, being
so restricted in life, you see the
vast barren desert where
nothing grows. It covers huge
tracts of land. You join a
caravan on the desert. So you
are travelling. Where are you
going? And is this the place in
which you wish to travel?

"It seems you answer those
questions for yourself by
seeing the journey in an
ancient mode. You see it like
the journey that people have
taken since Biblical times. In
that way it is an elemental
journey. It also suggests that
whatever your experiences,
you are in no way stuck. Your
response to your situation in
life is to move, and to join

others who are moving—a
very strong and wise response.

"On the practical side, the
spear through your right-hand
side is significant and I suspect
it is connected with your
practical worries. Your body
actually tilts to the right as you
meditate. I would guess you
are holding practical problems
in your body, which you should
address to prevent a physical
problem from developing. But
they may not be real, current,
practical problems. More than
anything they seem the
memory of practical problems
you have faced.

"It is also as if you are
holding yourself in a state
of anticipation 'just in case
something occurs.' It is not
necessary. You are strong,
constructive, wise, and
creative. Any sort of physical
movement, though, would be
good—dance, for example, or
swimming—to help avoid a
problem developing. It is
something you can easily
affect at this stage, you have
real access to yourself.

"Thank you for sharing your
journey. Go well."

"*Thank you.*"

"Max, you're next."

EMOTIONAL REALITY

"I saw a beautiful purple color. Something like a bird, an eagle——a big bird—appeared a few times. Then an eye. It was pleasant. But before that, it hadn't been. I saw something like the Edvard Munch picture of 'The Scream.' When that happened, I lost my concentration and had difficulty keeping my eyes closed.

"Then I felt something like a pain in my left side and I was worried that I was not doing what I should be doing. So I asked a question, 'What should I do?' and the answer was, 'Relax,' which was a real relief.

"And then I didn't really want to come back when you told us to, I just felt, 'I need to remind myself to relax.'"

"Thank you. You'd like me to say something?"

He nods

"The crucial point here is the picture, 'The Scream.' The instruction to go back into the place that you need to go takes you back to 'The Scream.' It says that in the inner world, what you feel is a scream, like the picture, and that scream is intolerable. And because the scream is intolerable, you look for guidance, or perhaps simply protection, from the purple. Purple is the color of the highest authority— royal purple—so you turn to it. You also turn to the eagle, another symbol of power, or even the mystical third eye, for help and protection.

"But unfortunately that doesn't work. Although it offers momentary relief, it doesn't take you anywhere. It might be of some use, but that inner scream is more powerful. It is the scream that you are first and foremost going to have to address. Help is available for all of us to guide us. But we need to take responsibility for addressing our situations and our problems. If you persevere you will find, metaphorically speaking, that light will shine for you, that light will show you the path you have to walk.

"When you walk the path you will be confronting the scream. The first instruction your own wisdom gives you is to relax. And it is tremendously helpful that you have such good and instantaneous access to your own wisdom in a tricky situation."

Where does it come from, this scream? From which part of me?"

"It's an expression of the inner forces within you. It's an emotional reality that is also a practical reality. The demands and the pressures that you are putting on yourself, as well as those you are facing and have faced from the outside, are creating a particular tension. You are holding that tension at a deep level in yourself. Looking at your energy, it's particularly evident at the sexual chakra. Though you are dealing with problems, and their consequences, particularly related to the areas the sexual chakra governs, you need to address those issues to help avoid physical problems developing and to move on emotionally. I suspect that the chakra meditation will be helpful to you in dealing with these pains and pressures. It's a big task, but you can do it. You have already started."

Yes. Thanks."

"Good. Tony."

GATEWAY THROUGH TIME

"When you asked us to start walking down the steps to begin with, mine went up. Only as I kept walking, they began to go down. At the bottom were a set of very large golden doors, which I opened—I seemed to be a child at this point—and as I opened the doors a great deal of light, and I think a few geese, flew out as well.

"Then I was in a Mediterranean landscape and I walked for a short period, and I remember bending down and allowing sand to run through my fingers.

"Later I saw a very rough sea at night and the top of a building, like a bungalow, just above the waves. Everything was almost black and then this big kind of sea monster came out, covered in seaweed and mud.

"Next the scene sort of shifted. I saw a kind of Pegasus horse, which flew by, and then I saw, very vaguely, a kind of nebulae of angelic forces in the far distance.

"The only thing I remember after that was a diagram of an inverted cone that seemed to be spinning, but it was very vague. All the images were very vague and I was aware of quite a lot of physical discomfort in the collarbone and my back and my leg."

"Thank you. Would you like me to speak about it?"

"Yes, please."

"What I am going to say comes from a great depth in me, so the words may be difficult, or the sense hard to understand.

"I suspect you are dealing with many issues in the present, and it is as if you made a decision to go forward in time. It's as if you decided, 'I don't want to connect with the present and I don't want to connect with the past, so I'll try to go forward.' Of course, in some ways going into the future brings rewards. But ultimately, of course, the future is part of the past. And, for a moment, you recaptured the wonder of being a child, opening the great gates, with so many possibilities and marvels.

"But then you find yourself at night at the seashore. Your emotions are very choppy, and in darkness. An emotional base, perhaps even a practical home, is largely submerged in your feelings—which means you don't have access to it, and cannot benefit from it.

"Then a monster emerges from the sea, it is the monster constructed from your own emotions, covered in seaweed and mud. Although you haven't yet decided how to resolve the present issues—the monster, and the issue of your base in particular—there are great and inspiring forces ahead too. Just remember you can't escape into the future without confronting the present, and there is considerable power available to help you do that.

"Thank you for sharing your visions."

"Thank you."

"Val, would you like to speak?"

GOING INTO THE INTERIOR

"I made myself go down the stairs. I didn't want to, but I managed to do it. When I got to the bottom, there were more stairs facing me. They were only partly lit. At the end was a door. I went through into a dark room with a fire burning in the fireplace and a table. But there was nothing else in the room. I thought, 'What am I doing?' There were windows, but you couldn't see anything out of them: They seemed to be covered in some way. So I left the room and went down another tunnel. At that point I realized I was in a cave in a huge cliff face. I was sitting on a ledge miles up this cliff, facing an enormous seascape. I think I tried flying! But I didn' really want to do that. I didn't know what I wanted. I gave up really, and I went back into the room where I started.

"Then something punched up into the ceiling of the room—some sort of energy just went PUNCH! And light poured through, masses of light.

"Suddenly I was really moving. I didn't know where I was going. I asked God where was I going. I was worried about my head. My head felt round like a balloon and there was a sense of yellow surrounding it. But it didn't feel in any way fixed, I just felt very light-headed, and my heart was beating very fast. I kept moving—going back into the room and then out again.

"Then I found myself in water. It was a greenish white color, and somehow light. It was very pleasant to be in the water. I felt like a young girl. I felt very 'floaty' and fluid.

"When finally I came out of the water, there were tall trees all around. I seemed to have gotten into a tree somehow, but then I kept on going. I found myself actually becoming one of these tall trees. The tops of the trees were masts of

ships. But when I noticed this, I was down on the ground again.

"The ground was covered with green moss, with a thicket of trees ahead. I kept going towards the thicket but I never got there. I don't think I wanted to, though I felt I should or maybe I would have to. My last image was of being in a little rowboat at dusk on misty water."

"Great. Do you want me to talk about it?"

"Please."

"In some ways you don't want to do this meditation. But obviously your desire to do it outweighs your desire not to do it, because you make yourself go down the stairs. And, it's interesting and important that you are actually able to go down the stairs. If you really didn't want to do the meditation, you would not be able to go anywhere.

"So, reluctantly, you go down to the room in your interior. You're fed up. You feel there is nothing of interest or importance there. All you see are a table, a fire, and windows you can't look out of. You don' want to go and explore—the whole experience does not seem rewarding to you.

"Finally you move down another tunnel—which means you go in another direction. You find yourself in a cave in a cliff face above the sea. You are high above the water. As always, the water is the emotional realm. It is quite out of reach. The place where you are doesn't sound like a particularly comfortable place.

"You think about flying. The air—the intellectual realm— is around you. But you don't really want to do that either. You are not at all clear about what you want, or your

mpetence. You seem to be frustrated and to lack
nfidence. Finally, you decide to go back into the
terior room. That is, into your own interior, despite
ur reluctance to face it and your belief that nothing
teresting is there.

"This is a wise step. You are accepting the need to
nfront yourself—your strengths, weaknesses, needs,
esires, and feelings. That willingness to go back into
e interior is a major step. You are deciding to face
hat is. The effect of doing so is the equivalent to the
of of the cave being, literally, punched through. It's
most like Divine intervention. Miraculously, you are
fered healing. The Forces that Be offer you healing.
he feeling of your head being manipulated is the
eling of being flooded by the Light. You are letting
e Light into yourself.

"Having been healed, you are then able to go out
to the emotional realm. You enter the water, which
els light and lovely. You float in the water—in other
ords, you are supported there. You feel much
ounger, cleaner, and able to move around. Not only
n you manage the water, but you can go on into the
rest of issues. There are many issues. You even see
em as great vessels, they're traveling and powerful,
ut that does not stop you.

"You keep moving. You are not trapped in one place
 fixated on an image, you are actually moving. You
e not held by one particular problem along the way.
ou are moving towards a thicket, where the issues are
acked particularly close. You don't really want to go
to the thicket, though you know you have to go there.
s fine to take things at a pace that feels comfortable.
ou certainly don't have to confront all your problems,
 weaknesses, at once—or until you feel ready.

"Finally, the last image shows that you are able to
ow down, to rest and deal with what is manageable:
 be in a little rowboat. It's important, too, that when
ou rest you are actually resting on water, emotion,
nd that it is not just manageable, but peaceful.

"Well done. Next is Jane."

MOVING VERY QUICKLY

"Things moved so quickly—there were so many images, but I'll try to reconstruct what I can. When you said, 'Go down,' I had a conscious image of going underneath a river. I felt I was going into somewhere very muddy. The first imag that came to me then was of hot bubbling water on a very primal surface. It was the kind of surfac I imagine you would expect to find on another planet. I thought, 'This is dangerous!' Then I thought, 'No, it's all right, I'm okay to be here.'

"As I watched, the surface continued bubbling away for a few seconds, but then it turned into something else It became an area of fountains, which looked sort of like palm trees. As I watched, the water from the fountains flowed over and became like rapids. I was in the water. I was being bounced down the flowing water and it was very stony. I thought, 'Oh gosh, isn't this going to hurt?' but immediately I felt, 'No, it's all right.' So I just bounced around. Then I realized that I was being held in a shape, in a way, and the shape was a circle. I thought that it was amusing. I've never gambled, but the circle looked like a roulette wheel, with a ball going click, click, click, click. I felt I was the ball, I was being bounced through the rapids.

"Again, I felt no pain. Things were changing very quickly. I turned into the shape of a worm and then I became a snake. It was all happening at great speed. Things were just whizzing by. Suddenly I became like a train going through a tunnel, the same shape whizzing through a tunnel and everything whizzing by me. And then I was somehow in a car, so I wasn't a train or a snake anymore.

"Next I came out onto a road, where I seemed to be human again. I was suddenly a young boy wearing a baseball cap, running around, kicking a soccer ball.

oon I was running really fast. The speed just seemed
o increase. I was running so fast I was actually pretty
much flying. Then there was an image of me as
a sort of bird, and I seemed to be going down at full
peed. And then I don't quite know what happened.
Except for one thing.

"When you suggested we come out, I was standing—
as a bird—on something that looked like a round saucer
in a very light blue color, but there was nothing in
the saucer. The sky around me was dark. I thought,
'Perhaps it is sunrise or sunset,' and just then you
said, 'As you come out, reality comes and it's night
and....' When I finally seemed to join with your
suggestions, I seemed to be on a road, a very dark flat
road with lots of traffic going by, and lights flashing by.
It was very confusing."

Thank you. Do you want me to talk about it?"

Yes, please."

It sounds as if, despite your desires, you are
not going to the place where your innermost
self wants to go. You start by crossing the river
into the unconscious. When you get there, it's
like molten mud with explosions coming up
from the emotions below and then fountains
of water pouring out. Interestingly, you don't
find any of that particularly threatening—and
I rather wonder: Why not? It's water exploding
out of molten mud—that could be rather
threatening. But it seems as if in a way you've
suspended yourself and your feelings, as if
you are saying, 'I will not respond to this.'
Instead, you quicken the pace. You choose
to pass through events very quickly.

"When you reach the worm that becomes
the snake, it is an image for the energy that
is rising inside you. It could tell you what's
happening, or take you further into yourself.
But you do not want to stay to allow it to
develop, which would be hard to hear. You are

moving too quickly—you can't be slow and still,
you continue on your speedy way. You travel:
You become a train into the tunnel, but it never
reaches its destination because it becomes a car.
Then the car changes.

"At this point your unconscious breaks through
to show you yourself as a boy wearing a baseball
cap. You are human for the first time. There is
something here that you really have to listen to.
But you don't. Even though you've slowed down
for the boy and the knowledge of the boy to come
to you, you soon move on again. You continue
moving until you become a creature of the air,
the bird.

"The air can represent the mental realm, which
I think it does here. It is a way of saying, 'You are
purely mental now.' But even as the bird, the
desire for inner nourishment, for meaning and
understanding, is very strong. The bird goes to
the saucer. Saucers are often put out with water
or food for small animals or pets. The bird stands
on a saucer, it goes to the source of nourishment,
but it's empty. There is nothing in the saucer.

"The meditation suggests that, like it or not,
you will go into yourself and you will hear what
that boy, and whoever else, has to say. But at the
moment, there is a tussle going on with your own
unconscious, which doesn't really want to stop
and listen.

"Very well done. You share many issues with
Tony. You might find working or talking together
useful.

"Bob, would you like to talk about your
experiences?"

THE NEED TO REST

"It felt as if I was trying to see images, but I wasn't really letting myself – or able to – see images spontaneously. Three images did come up. In the first, I was walking in a forest and the path became very muddy. Then I was on the top of a cliff and the weather was very strong. This cliff-top place felt familiar. The last image was of walking into the sea and becoming a fish, then going down into the ocean, but not being able to follow the fish any farther down.

"And all along, there was a very strong feeling of pressure and a sense of concentration on my forehead. I seemed more aware of that than anything else."

"Would you like me to speak about your meditation?" He *nods.*

"You are very tired, and you probably know that. Your body is not strong enough. You want to do the meditation but your physical vehicle – your body – isn't strong enough at the moment. The only prescription is rest, which will work wonders.

"The pressure on your forehead is the vision trying to get through to you. But because you are so tired right now, you can't hold it. Rest. The meditation tells you all this. You are a little lost on the forest path, and you are in a rather exposed place in life, probably being buffeted by what you call 'strong weather'. You are happy to explore the emotional issues involved, to become the fish and go into the sea, but you can't follow at the moment. Take a rest. Don't tire yourself. There is no need for hurry. All that you need to happen will happen in its own time. You are not blocking it. You're just tired! Rest."

"Thank you."

"Alex, would you like to say anything?"

LOCKING OUT DIFFICULTIES

"Well, I felt like I slept for the most part. And then when I woke up, I was in a cave. It was a dark, black cave, and there was a man chained to the wall of the cave with a thick, old, heavy chain. And then it dissipated, or I dissipated. And that's it."

"Thank you. Do you want me to talk about it?"

"Sure. I wasn't very thrilled, I have to say. I feel very sad."

"What your meditation is saying is that despite your aspirations you are here because you want to be – your body and some part of you haven't settled into this process yet, or aren't ready to participate fully yet. Perhaps you thought it was a different process from what it actually is...? You probably also thought that it was a less demanding process than it is. Because you are very capable professionally, perhaps you thought this sort of meditation would be no trouble to master. But this process requires very different qualities from those you use in your professional life. Being a high achiever at work does not necessarily mean that you find this easy to do in the beginning. "You probably also felt physical discomfort during the exercise. It's not surprising that you feel as if you are going to sleep. It's a way of trying to block out the difficulties of the situation. The image of the cave, with the man chained to the wall, suggests that is how you see or feel about yourself and your issues. Of course it makes you feel sad, especially if you feel unable to unchain the man.

"It's as if you respond to your meditation by saying to yourself, 'Here I am, back again with these old issues. I don't want to know them anymore. I don't want to be back in this place.' But the fact is that you will be back in this place until you have resolved some of the issues it poses and so are ready to move on. Simply wanting to move on is the start, but not quite enough to make it happen. It requires effort. And it also requires humility to accept your human frailties and weaknesses, and to recognize yourself as part of humanity. That is important. It can be a hard lesson. Well done for making a start. Thank you for sharing.

"Nancy, your turn, if you'd like to say anything?"

THE PAIN OF OTHERS

"To begin with, the words you were speaking seemed quite perfunctory. Then when you said, 'Go down and go through the trap door,' I couldn't do it. The door was really heavy, but it was also somehow swirling around. I had an overwhelming desire to sleep – but I fought it. Fragments kept coming up from the day, but they seemed random. My head was very heavy and I couldn't seem to go anywhere.

"Then I thought, 'Is this like before?' In the past, whenever emotional stuff has come up in the past and I haven't wanted to look at it, I've felt this incredible desire to sleep, to get away from it. But I can't be sure. Then I really heard the words, 'The trapdoor's closed, you can't go through.' Sometimes I think it's self-indulgent of me to think so much about myself, to want to understand things.

"Finally, just before the end, I remembered what you said about connecting with those who feel shame and hurt in the world. You spoke about feeling compassion for them, and through doing that, connecting with yourself and your own shame and hurt. Suddenly things came into focus. I saw a couple I met today and I saw where they were hurting, and I really felt for them. At that moment, I felt my heart really spread out and my head lifted and became lighter. I realized it was so important to look out at others rather than just look in. Or that's what it seemed like, but then we had reached the end."

"Good, thank you, Nancy. Do you want me to talk about your meditation?"

"Yes, please."

"I think that you're right when you recognize that you couldn't go through the trapdoor and face the emotional issues behind it. Facing emotional issues is not just a question of self-indulgence, which part of you might think.

"The very important aspect of your meditation, though, was being able to connect with the pain of others. You really felt for, and with, the couple you spoke of. The next step of course is realizing that you, too, carry pain and shame. It's crucial to see others' hurt and pain, but also to recognize that you carry the same qualities. It allows you to realize that you are not alone – we all suffer. At the same time, it shows you that others are like you – they hurt, too. Then, we all have to deal with our own individual situations, what some people call our own karma, in esoteric language. But we also have to deal with the collective, with the situation of our universe and everyone who lives there – what is sometimes called the group karma.

"When you understand how we are all linked, you understand that you cannot be well unless you are satisfied that you are doing your best for all others and our universe. In some cases, people find it difficult to deal with their own internal issues, in others they do not want to recognize anyone else's suffering. Ultimately, it's essential to be able to embrace both. Today you were connecting with the pain and shame of others."

"And can doing that help to open my heart?"

"Yes, indeed. Because you can see pain and suffering in them, it can ultimately enable you to admit and release the pain and suffering in you. Of course, what can happen is that you defend against your own pain by refusing to admit it, and instead concentrate only on others' pain. If that happens, you are saying, 'I'm fine; it's someone else who is hurting or has problems.' But I am sure you're not doing that, Nancy. Recognizing others' pain is also a wonderful way to access your own compassion. Thank you.

"Anna, do you want to say anything?"

FORGET YOURSELF

"Just very confused with cloudy, unclear images. I stepped forward and then I stepped backwards. Then I went through a door of some sort. I ended up in a white bare room. There was nothing in it apart from a huge worm that had been chopped up. It was all brown and gooey inside. But at the same time it was also rocky-like. Then it moved away, somehow, but it left bits of goo behind.

"Then I was in a forest. There was a very definite path, which wound round and went up a hill, and then down the other side. I was trying to follow it, but somehow I couldn't see it. Then I found it, but it was going in a different direction. Around that time I realized the forest was like a caricature of a forest, a fairytale forest. But then I realized that everything in it was actually static—nothing moved except me. Everything else was still.

"At some point I had a sense of different colors coming towards me: a greenish-blue and a yellow. Then I saw a room that seemed like a religious sanctuary, with many different images. When you asked us to come back, it was quite clear and I felt very nice coming up the stairs. But then I couldn't actually find myself here in this room. I saw everyone back in the room, but I was still somewhere else, just saying, 'Oh.' I knew I needed to come back but I didn't really want to. Then I had an image of myself in this chair but my mind was somehow outside the image. Finally, I managed to kind of come back in again. I felt a bit dozy."

"Thank you, Anna. Would you like my comments?"

She nods.

"There's only one thing you have to do and that's give. At the moment, your energy has been awakened—that's the serpent shape—but you are busy trying to make it do or be something. Not allowing it simply to take you where it needs to take you.

"What it's saying to you is, 'Forget yourself, concentrate on opening your heart and giving.' Don't look for images; don't look for things to happen. For the moment, just give up. That's all. And by just giving, it will allow that serpent to straighten itself out and then whatever images you need, they will come. Thank you.

"Well done, everybody."

Group meditation sessions always close in a particular format which helps the energy settle, and makes sure everyone leaves feeling calm and well. So with everyone sitting quietly, I speak again.

"Now focus your attention above. See the Blue Light as it moves in a clockwise direction. Know the blue rays have penetrated your body, bringing you healing and well-being. Capture the sensation, the precious gift, and let the light fade slowly as it pulls away from you. The effects will remain.

"Now the White Light burns alone as it moves in a counter-clockwise direction. It is your life, as it is the Light within you. Now let it recede from you as it fades into the atmosphere. An arrow made of White Light descends. It passes through your body, starting at your head: It passes through once; twice; three times. You are well and utterly present, replete, and filled with love of God and Man."

Healing is about becoming whole. Many

excellent books discuss healing and many

routes lead to healing. In essence, healing

is about allowing love into your life and

coming to know the reality of love. Love

transforms all realities and actions. For

example, knowing real love makes it

impossible to want to hurt others

or to turn in pain against oneself.

HEALING

the same way, love transforms the quality of each and every experience. It is about our heart being made whole, but that is not the same as the body being rid of all signs of illness. or the same as a cloak of invulnerability enveloping the emotions. In energetic terms, healing is about releasing the obstacles lodged in the body's energy, though the scars may remain. This is why meditation is such a powerful tool in healing. In the physical body those scars may continue to be present as actual physical limitations —an organ that is damaged beyond complete repair or a system that needs continual care. But that should not in any way be perceived as evidence of failure.

VALLEY

This picture brings a sense of tranquility and healing to me.

Ultimately, the life of the physical body may be over, the individual may face death, yet healing may be complete.

Healing is not about attaining and maintaining perfect physical health. It is about restoring the physical body to the maximum degree of wholeness of which it is capable—and its capabilities are often astonishing. Physical bodies can be limited by expectations of all sorts. But beyond the physical vehicle, healing is about restoring wholeness to the totality of the human being, including the finer energetic bodies: the emotional, intellectual, and spiritual bodies. In achieving that end, the power of love is the most potent of all forces.

GUIDED HEALING JOURNEY

Some years ago, I worked regularly with a group. Each member was a highly capable professional, and our sessions varied from heated intellectual debates to mystical teachings. We explored many areas together, and a great deal of healing took place. It was an enormously rich and enjoyable experience.

The folowing words are taken from a transcript of one of our mystical sessions, at the end of a year. We are seated in a circle, with the usual candles alight. The session started with a prayer, then I continued to lead a healing meditation. The words do not follow a strictly rational pattern, but flow in some other way.

Many of the scenes and experiences in meditation journeys have the quality of this image.

Now feel the bands that immediately and instantly have established themselves between us here. Feel how the current runs in a counterclockwise direction, as I sit at the head of this circle. Feel the rays that shine from us to join with others around the universe. Feel the way this point of light that we form glows. Feel how the beams radiate from us, to encompass each and every other on the planet. Feel the way the quality we are offering from this place extends to other dimensions. And feel joy. Feel pleasure at what it is that we can give. Feel pleasure and immense pride at what it is that we can receive. Be glad to be one.

"Acknowledge your achievements to yourself, in a true sense. Not in a sense that seeks to put others below you, but in a sense that acknowledges the steps you have made. Feel pleased and proud at the place that you stand in. Acknowledge yourself for the work you have done. Know that at the same time there is everything and nothing still to do. And be joyful, peaceful, and pleased.

"Allow the year to end and the next to begin. Allow death where it calls. Shed the skin. Die where necessary. Let the end begin. Let the ends that have begun proceed. Let yourself be no longer, for it matters not. You will continue, you will rise again, you will be born afresh and anew. You will be led. Follow where you are led."

GUIDED HEALING JOURNEY

Now, concentrate on opening your hearts. Concentrate on giving from the depths of your being. Give to the group first of all. We will hold each member of the group in mind individually, and offer to that person. So, to begin with, place Robert in your minds, and to his image give your love, not to any specific part of him, but simply to his image offer your love and healing. Robert, ask for light for yourself.

Hold Robert in mind now, and simultaneously hold your heart open. Feel the joy, the love, pride, and pleasure of giving.

And now, wish Robert well, and replace his image with that of Ken.

Again, Ken ask for light for yourself, draw it down. Give Ken love. Feel the beams radiating from your heart. Feel the heart chakra growing wider and wider. It glows as the sun and moon, and as the earth itself.

Now wish Ken well, and replace his image with that of Nathan. Offer your love, and your wisdom too -- everything that you have, give to Nathan, to build his strength and sense of unity.

Wish Nathan well and replace his image with that of Rose. Rose, ask for the Light, for beneficence, for all you most desire.

And the rest of us, hold Rose to our hearts. Offer her the gifts that come from our very souls that she may be healed, which is to become whole in every way she can.

Offer Rose love, and wish her well, and replace her image with that of Barbara. To Barbara give your love. To Barbara open your heart and ask that the earth may be hers, and may be as heaven. Barbara, turn to the light and accept. Feel that chakra as it stretches wider and wider, to places you never knew you were capable of reaching. Allow yourself to give with all your heart.

And wish Barbara well, and replace her image with that of Ruth.

Ruth, pull down the light, as you need it. The rest of us, turn your hearts to Ruth and open them to allow your gifts to shine for Ruth. Give all that you can, and you will be given to in return. Now give your love to Ruth.

Wish Ruth well, and replace her image with that of me. Again offer your love, give your hearts as you will.

Now wish me well, and turn to the threads that bind the group. See the energy, the love that flows between us as it flows in a clockwise direction around the group. Hold that knowledge of love. Feel it as it moves up your spine, to the back of your neck, the most rigid part of the body, and over your head to the front part of your brain, illuminating all.

You are at the highest point of which you are capable, for now. You are able to hold that condition, that awareness, that love, in reality -- so that you do not know it only here, but allow it to form a portion of your everyday functioning. Hold it to integrate it.

Then open your eyes, and reconnect with the present, with love."

We finished with a prayer of thanks, and much joy.

MEDITATION IN LIFE

Sometimes people ask whether the visions and the reality I have known in meditation are still accessible to me. The answer is "Yes," although I no longer have to see the visions or experience an altered state of reality to produce the same results. Today, silent meditation is not my main practice. Meditation in life is more important to me.

On occasions, when it is appropriate, I help others to see and understand their own visions, whether they occur in meditation, dreams, or simply as a sense in life. At the same time, I keep the route to creativity, which is the continuation of the route to meditation, as open as I can, and enjoy the consequences. My reality is interwoven with the consciousness that meditation has brought. It informs and transforms my experience. To the best of my ability, I practice meditation in everyday life.

"Meditation in life" is a Buddhist expression. For me, it means holding on, in everyday life, to the sensitivity, openness, and equilibrium that meditation brings. The chakra meditation practice is enormously valuable for the effects that it can produce. It is not desirable as a source of exotic or out of the world experiences. It has the power to dramatically alter the body's energy, which has consequences for feelings, intellectual understanding, and physical reality. Changes that occur in all these areas lead to greater awareness, expanded energy, a real sense of peace, and power too, in the everyday. Beyond that, the chakra meditation brings the ability to hold on to those changes in life.

At each energy level, practicing the meditation reinforces the changes it creates. Repeated practice deepens and strengthens the effects. Ultimately, though, the purpose of the meditation is to enable the awareness it promotes and the open-hearted, informed condition it seeks to

stablish as part of everyday life. The exercise
f holding on to these states and the power they
roduce is no more and no less than meditation
ı the everyday.

Today I work a great deal with professionals,
ıcluding leaders in the business world,
ntertainment celebrities, psychotherapists and
thers. For them, as for everyone, my meditation
ıethod, consultations, and seminars are a route
ɔ a greater understanding of self: a route to the
eepest self. They are also a path to a wider, wiser
wareness of the world and the place of each in it.

This is a path that aims to bring the ability to
live this perspective in everyday life. Working with
people, I want to develop their sense of self and
their comprehension of the world, and by doing so,
their ability to work and live at the highest level.
These aims are met by strengthening joy, creativity,
and peace—and by bringing understanding of the
true nature of power, including the power of love.

shua Tree in California
a place where the
editation states and
e come very close.
ccess to the deepest
lf is easy.

REFERENCES

American Association of Music
Therapy website
www.musictherapy.org

Berendt, Joachim-Ernst
Nada Brahma: The World Is Sound
(Rochester, Vermont: Destiny Books,
1987)

Burckhardt, Jacob
The Civilization of the Renaissance in Italy
Translated by S. G. Middlemore
(Viking Penguin, 1990)

Chan, Linda
"Critical Care Nurse"
International Journal of Rehabilitation
(June 1, 1999)

Chopra, Deepak
Grow Younger, Live Longer
(Rider, 2001)

Chopra, Deepak
How to Know God
(Rider, 2000)

Clark, Kenneth
Civilisation
(Harper & Row, 1970)

Cochran, Lin
*Edgar Cayce on Secrets of the Universe
and How to Use Them in Your Life*
(Warner Books, 1989)

Creighton, James, and Carl Simonton
Getting Well Again
(Bantam, 1992)

*Dakini Teachings: Padmasambhava's
Oral Instructions to Lady Tsogyal*
(Boston: Shambhala Publications,
1990)

Dalai Lama, Tenzin Gyatso
*The Meaning of Life from
a Buddhist Perspective*
Edited and translated by
Jeffrey Hopkins
(MA: Wisdom Publications, 1993)

Dalai Lama, Tenzin Gyatso
*The World of Tibetan Buddhism: An
Overview of Its Philosophy and Practice*
Edited and translated by
Geshe T. Jinpa
(MA: Wisdom Publications, 1995)

Daniel, Mark Haynes
World of Risk
(John Wiley & Sons, 2000)

Davidson, John
Subtle Energy
(Essex, England: The C.W.
Company Ltd, 1993)

Dossey, Larry, M.D.
*Meaning and Medicine: A Doctor's Tales
of Breakthrough and Healing*
(Bantam, 1992)

ossey, Larry, M.D.
einventing Medicine
Harper San Francisco, 1999)

ryer, H.
our Defense Against Cancer
Harper Collins, 1994)

euerstein, George
tructures of Consciousness
California: Integral Publishing,
995)

ershon, Michael D.
he Second Brain
HarperCollins, 1999)

oleman, Daniel
motional Intelligence
Bantam, 1995)

reen, Elmer and Alyce Green
eyond Biofeedback
Knoll Publishing, 1989)

Ching, or Book of Changes
ranslated by C. F. Baynes
nd Richard Wilhelm
Princeton University Press, 1967)

acob, Tim
Alpha Wave Content of EEG in
esponse to Aromatherapy Oils School
Biosciences"
Cardiff University)

Seasonal Affective Disorder"
urnal of the American Medical Association
December 1993)

Khan, Sufi Inayat
The Development of Spiritual Healing
(Hunter House, 1988)

Lad, Usha and Dr. Vashant Lad
Ayurvedic Cooking for Self-Healing
(Albuquerque, New Mexico:
The Ayurvedic Press, 1997)

Lawless, Julia
Encyclopaedia of Essential Oils: A Complete
Guide to the Use of Aromatics in Aromatherapy,
Herbalism, Health and Well-Being
(Element Books, 1992)

Levin, Michal
The Pool of Memory
(Dublin: Gill & Macmillan, 1998)

Levin, Michal
Spiritual Intelligence
(London: Hodder and Stoughton,
2000)

Liberman, Jacob
Light: Medicine of the Future:
How We Can Use It to Heal Ourselves
(Bear and Co., 1991)

McCraty, R. and M. Atkinson
"The Electricity of Touch"
Evolution of a New Paradigm of Science
and Inner Experience
(Boulder, CO: ISSSEEM, 1996)

Michio Kushi and Alex Jack
The Book of Macrobiotics
(Japan Publications, 1987)

Motoyama, Hiroshi
Theories of the Chakras
(Theosophical Publishing House, 1988)

Scholes, Percy A. and Denis Arnold
New Oxford Companion to Music
(Oxford University Press, 1983)

Ohsawa, George
The Book of Judgement
(George Ohsawa Macrobiotic Foundation)

Plato
The Dialogues of Plato
Edited by Justin Kaplan
Translated by Benjamin Jowett
(PB, 1984)

Reed, Henry
Edgar Cayce on Mysteries of the Mind
(Warner Books, 1989)

Saint Augustine
Confessions
Translated by Henry Chadwick
(Oxford University Press, 1998)

Schultz, Mona Lisa
Uncovering Intuition
(Three Rivers Press,1998)

Schwartz, Gary
The Living Energy Universe
(Hampton Roads, 1999)

Schwartz, Gary E. R. and Linda G. S. Russek
"Energy Cardiology, A Dynamic Energy
Systems Approach for Integrating
Conventional and Alternative Medicine"
Journal of Mind Body Health, 12, No 4
(Fall 1996)

Sheldrake, Rupert
*Dogs That Know When Their
Owners Are Coming Home and
Other Unexplained Powers of Animals*
(Crown Publishing Group, 1999)

Steiner, Rudolf
Colour
(London: R. Steiner Press, 1997)

Tarnas, Richard
*The Passion of the Western
Mind: Understanding The Ideas
That Have Shaped Our World View*
(London: Random House, 1996)

Tiller, William A.
Science and Human Transformation
(California: Pavior Publishing, 1997)

Wall, Vicky
The Miracle of Color Healing
(UK: Aquarian Press, 1990)

Wilber, Ken
A Brief History of Everything
(Boston: Shambhala, 1996)

Wilber, Ken
The Essential Ken Wilber
(Boston: Shambhala, 1998)

Wilber, Ken
Grace and Grit
(Boston: Shambhala: 1993)

Zukav, Gary
The Seat of the Soul
(St. Martins, 1990)

FURTHER RESOURCES

The following list includes contact information for organizations that offer instruction and seminars on meditation and other spiritual topics. Readers may want to contact these organizations directly with queries about specific services they provide.

Michal Levin works as a Personal Development Consultant and intuitive with companies and individuals in the USA and UK. Instructors she has trained also teach the chakra meditation described in this book. To contact her please e-mail: enquiries@MichalLevin.com.

Michal's website address is: www.MichalLevin.com.

California Institute of Integral Studies
1453 Mission Street
San Francisco, CA 94103
(415)575-6100
info@ciis.edu

The Chopra Center for Well-Being
7630 Fay Avenue
LaJolla, CA 92037
(858)551-7788

Esalen Institute
Big Sur, CA
(831)667-3000
www.esalen.org

Institute of Noetic Sciences
101 San Antonio Road
Petaluma, CA 94952
(707)781-7420

Omega Institute
150 Lake Drive
Rhineland, NY 12572
(800)944-1001

INDEX

PICTURE CREDITS

The publishers would like to thank the following for their kind permission to reproduce the photographs and artworks:

CORBIS: Half title page **Optical Artists**; title page **Andy Kassab**; contents background **Rick Doyle**; contents, candles **Mark Thiessen**; contents, sunrise **First Light**; contents, trees **Patrick W. Stoll**; contents, fish **Stephen Frink**; pages 14-15 **Phil Schermeister**; page 18 **Macduff Everton**; page 23, bottom **Marc Muench**; pages 24-25 **Galvin Wickham**; pages 28-29 **Sheldan Collins**; page 30 **Brian Vikander**; page 35 **Kevin Fleming**; page 36, left **Owen Franken**; page 39, top left **Alexander Burkatowski**; page 39, top right **Reuters New Media Inc.**; page 39, bottom left **Kevin Dodge**; page 39, bottom right **Bob Krist**; page 42, left **Corbis**; page 42 **Archivo Iconografico, S.A.**; page 43, top left **Bettmann**; page 43, bottom left **David & Peter Turnley**; page 43, top right **Flip Schulke**; page 43, bottom right **Philip Gould**; page 44 **Bruce Burkhardt**; pages 44-45 **Archivo Iconografico, S.A.**; page 46, left **Laura Paresky**; page 46, right **Bohemian Nomad Picturemakers**; page 47 **Dean Conger**; page 0 **Corbis**; page 54 **Ariel Skelley**; pages 54-55 **Anthony Nex**; page 57 top **Bettmann**; pages 58-59 **Chris Collins**; page 59, top **Bill Varie**; pages 60-61 **Photo Library International**; page 62, bottom **Rob Lewine**; pages 62-63 **Robbie Jack**; page 64 **Bettmann**; page 64-65 **Lindsay Hebberd**; page 66 **Ralph A. Clevenger**; pages 68-69 **Michael Busselle**; page 72 **Valentine Atkinson**; page 73 **Richard T. Nowitz**; page 4, right **David & Peter Turnley**; page 75 **Lindsay Hebberd**; pages 76-77 **David Samuel Robbins**; page 8 **Paul A. Souders**; page 80 left **Michael S. Yamashita**; page 80 right **William Sallaz/Duomo**; page 2, left **Richard Hamilton, Smizth**; page 82, right **Jim Zuckerman**; page 83 **Robert Holmes**; page 98 **Bill Varie**; page 95 **Jean-Pierre Lescourret**; pages 100-101 **First Light**; page 102 **D. Boone**; page 104, left **John W. Herbst**; page 104, right **Peter Johnson**; pages 104-105 **Raymond Gehman**; page 106, left **Massimo Listri**; page 106, right **Ted Spiegel**; page 107 **Sheldan Collins**; pages 108-109 **Don Hammond**; page 112 **Richard Hamilton Smith**; pages 112-113 **Mark Thiessen**; pages 114-115; pages 116-117 **Digital Art**; page 118 **Kevin T. Gilbert**; pages 118-119 **Digital Art**; page 119 **Eye Ubiquitous**; page 120 **Michael Boys**; page 121 **Darrell Gulin**; page 122 **Eric & David Hosking**; page 123, top **Marc Garanger**; page 123, bottom **Bettmann**; page 124 **Patrick W. Stoll**; page

125, top **Niall Benvie**; page 125, bottom **Douglas Peebles**; page 126, top **Bill Ross**; page 126, bottom **Jeff Vanuga**; page 128, top **D. Robert & Lorri Franz**; page 128, bottom **Craig Aurness**; page 129 **Burstein Collection**; page 130 **Jonathan Blair**; page 131, top **Dave Bartruff**; page 131, bottom **David Martinez**; pages 132-133 **Darrell Gulin**; page 133, top **James Davis/Eye Ubiquitous**; page 133, bottom **Bob RowanProgressive Image**; page 134, top **D. Robert & Lorri Franz**; page 134, bottom **Robert Young Pelton**; page 136, top **Patrick W. Stoll**; page 136, bottom **Stephen Frink**; page 137 **Robert Holmes**; page 139, face **Lumenstock**; page 139, doves **Annie Griffiths Belt**; page 140 **Gian Berto Vanni/Vanni Archive**; page 141 **Digital Art**; page 144 **Brad Miller**; pages 144-145 **Pablo Corral Vega**; page 146 **Guy Motil**; page 147 **Peter Johnson**; page 148 **Pat O'Hara**; page 149 **Hubert Stadler**

MICHAL LEVIN: Contents page; pages 8-13 backgrounds; page 11; page 13; pages 16-7; page 19; page 22; page 25; page 36, right; page 38; pages 40-41; pages 50-51; page 54; page 56; page 58; page 60; page 62; page 64; page 66; pages 70-71; pages 84-85; page 90; pages 96-97; page 98-99; page 100; page 103; pages 110-111; pages 142-143

DIANA CATHERINES: Page 27; page 53; page 55; page 57 bottom right; page 59 bottom right; page 61; page 63; page 65; page 67; page 87; pages 88-89; page 91; pages 92-93

DORLING KINDERSLEY LTD: Page 32, left; page 33, left **Roger Phillips**; page 33, center; page 33, top right **Matthew Ward**; page 33, bottom; page 34, communion cup **Andy Crawford/National Museums of Scotland**; page 34, bread; page 56-57 **Mark Harwood**; page 74, left **Dave King**; page 79 **Dave King**

ADDITIONAL SOURCES: Page 20 **Mehau Kulyk/Science Photo Library**; page 21 **Dr. Wm. M. Harlow**; page 23, top **Klaus Aarsleff/Fortean Picture Library**; page 31 **Janet & Colin Bord/Fortean Picture Library**; page 32, right **Jose L. Pelaez Inc/Stock Market**; page 48, left **Bridgeman Art Library**; page 52 **Ancient Art & Architecture Collection Ltd**; page 138 **Image Bank**

DK Publishing has endeavored to credit each source correctly. If anyone can provide additional information regarding these sources, please contact DK Publishing.

ACKNOWLEDGEMENTS

Where to begin? This book is the work of such a wide range of forces—people, places, and presences—all contributed their energies. Among those to whom I owe particular thanks are my infinitely generous and inspired son and daughter, Tom and Eleanor, love everlasting to you both. Profound thanks and love to my wonderful mother, Leah Levin.

My thanks also to my many clients, old and new—we have exchanged so much. There are far too many names to recount, but Sue Arnold, David Lewis, Janet Morris, Ruthie Smith, Neil Spencer, Anne Robinson, Rosalyn Ward, Caroline Ward, and Kolinka Zinovieff have been especially generous.

To other friends and colleagues, including Barnet Bain, Alexander Cheetham, Rev. Colin Hodgetts, Brian Hilliard and Arielle Ford, James Hood, Dr. Kim Jobst, Scilla Thomas, Felicity and Alex Duncan, The Earl and Countess of Portsmouth, Anna Maria Rossi, Dr. Alan Watkins, Nick Segal, and my excellent agent Clare Alexander, who have supported my endeavors and shared theirs with me—thank you. Special thanks, too, to Ken Wilber. May we all continue to play our parts in the cosmic dance to the best of our ability.

Then, to the landscapes, cityscapes, flora, and fauna who have wooed me, my awe and devotion. To all the forces of the deeper dimensions, as always, my complete allegiance. May I continue to grow in understanding along with the ability to act in harmony with that understanding.

Next, to my publishers, Christopher Davis in London, LaVonne Carlson and Mandy Earey in New York, who along with their teams worked so hard to give this book its form, a great thank you. And finally, to Bob Richards —thank you for everything.

DK Publishing would like to thank Chris Avgherinos, Diana Catherines, Russell Shaw and Tina Vaughan for all their patience and hard work; Martin Copeland, Mark Dennis, Hanna Edwards, Mariana Sonnenberg, Louise Thomas, and Jo Walton for picture research; Katherine Yam and her team at Colourscan for all the help reproducing this book, Nanette Cardon for the thorough index; and Lisa Cupido and Raj Mankad for their invaluable assistance.